The SECRETS *of* TANTRIC BUDDHISM

The SECRETS *of* TANTRIC BUDDHISM

Understanding the Ecstasy of Enlightenment

THOMAS CLEARY

JAICO PUBLISHING HOUSE

Ahmedabad Bangalore Chennai
Delhi Hyderabad Kolkata Mumbai

Published by Jaico Publishing House
A-2 Jash Chambers, 7-A Sir Phirozshah Mehta Road
Fort, Mumbai - 400 001
jaicopub@jaicobooks.com
www.jaicobooks.com

Published in arrangement with
Red Wheel/Weiser, LLC
65, Parker St. Unit 7
Newburyport, MA 01950, USA

THE SECRETS OF TANTRIC BUDDHISM
ISBN 978-81-8495-905-5

First Jaico Impression: 2016

Printed by
Repro India Limited, Mumbai

This work is dedicated to the memory of the honorable Abdul Aziz, former Senior Advocate of the Supreme Court of Bangladesh.

"Exemplary people understand things in terms of justice."
—Analects of Confucius

CONTENTS

ORIGINS OF TANTRIC BUDDHISM

Tantrism is widely known as the most elaborate and colorful form of Buddhism. It is considered by many to be the most sophisticated form of Buddhism, while viewed by some as the most degenerate. It is certainly the most controversial. In modern times, Tantrism is the principal mode of Buddhism in Tibet, Nepal, Bhutan, Ladakh, and Mongolia, as well as a major tradition of Buddhism in Japan.

In the past, Tantric Buddhism was also practiced in India and China, and probably in what are now Afghanistan, Indonesia, and Malaysia. Tantrism was absorbed by Taoism in China, by Hinduism and Sufism in India, by Sufism in Afghanistan, and by Hinduism and Sufism in Indonesia and Malaysia.

The main source of Tantric Buddhism, from which the movement emanated over such a vast area of Asia, was the extraordinarily rich cultural basin of old Bengal. Now comprising Bangladesh and part of India, the Bengal region was just east of Magadha, the original homeland of Buddhism. A major center of trade since ancient times, the Bengali cultural basin was connected with many different regions, including the Greek and Roman spheres, by both land and sea routes. It is one of the oldest strongholds of Buddhism.

Numerous ethnic and linguistic groups have inhabited the region of old Bengal since ancient times, and many more were to immigrate there over the ages. This process resulted in a diverse population, with many different traditions of thought and behavior. When Bengal was eventually integrated into Aryan and Muslim polities, this endemic cultural pluralism survived, engendering a spirit of religious tolerance that withstood even the most violent political agitations and pressures. There can hardly be any doubt that Tantrism played a major role in this aspect of Bengali cultural resilience. The Buddhist presence in Bengal was very old and well established when Tantrism emerged as a distinct movement. According to the famous seventh-century Chinese pilgrim Hsuan-tsang, Gautama Buddha, himself, visited several places in Bengal and taught there. While there is no concrete corroboration of this claim, it cannot be considered unlikely.

There is, after all, no surviving concrete contemporaneous corroboration of anything about Buddhism in the lifetime of Buddha himself. There was no Buddhist art in Buddha's time, and no Buddhist literature. But it is well established that Buddha did travel around during nearly fifty years of teaching activity, and Bengal was a highly accessible neighbor to Buddha's native Magadha. The linguistic differences between the majority languages of Magadha and Bengal were at most dialectical.

Even if Gautama Buddha himself did not visit Bengal personally, given the status of Bengal as a trade center, and the known support for Buddhism among the merchant class in India, it would seem reasonable to consider it likely that Buddhism did, indeed, enter the Bengali region from very early times.

The first concrete monumental evidence of Buddhist presence in Bengal appears to be a stone plaque inscription assigned to the Maurya period (c. 325–183 B.C.E.). Two votive inscriptions on the railing of a Buddhist stupa are dated from the second century B.C.E. According to the Buddhist historian Taranatha, Buddhist communities were established in east Bengal from the time of the great Maurya emperor Ashoka (c. 273–232 B.C.E.).

Ashoka united nearly all of India, including Baluchistan and Afghanistan, under the Maurya rule. He is known to have sent Buddhist missionaries all over the Indian subcontinent, as far south as Sri Lanka, and as far west as Anatolia, Syria, Egypt, and Greece. Considering the fact that Buddhism is even believed to have reached as far as Ireland at this time, via the sea route from the Mediterranean, it is hardly thinkable that Bengal would not have been within the scope of this vast missionary effort.

Early Buddhist literature, although of uncertain date because of its derivation from oral tradition, mentions Bengal as a center of maritime trade and of Buddhist activity from olden times. The *Mahavamsa* refers to a prince named Vijaya who made a voyage from Bengal to Sri Lanka with a retinue of seven hundred. The *Mahaniddesa* acknowledges Bengal as an important center of overseas trade, and so does the remarkable *Milindapanho, Questions of Menander,* which is believed to record conversations of a Buddhist elder with a Graeco-Buddhist king. It is well known that Buddhism spread through Central Asia and into China along the Silk Road trade routes, and there can hardly be any doubt that knowledge of Buddhism also went along with other forms of international communication in other regions as well.

The dialogue with Menander would have taken place in the West, on the other side of the Indian subcontinent, where the empire of Alexander the Great collided with that of Chandragupta Maurya. Mention in this context would reflect the farflung fame of Bengal in those ancient times. The *Divyavadana* also includes north Bengal within the domain of the Buddhist *majjimadesa* or "Middle Country," the classical homeland of Buddhism.

The reputation of old Bengali Buddhism becomes even clearer in the early centuries of the common era. An inscription dated back to the second or third century includes Vanga, in the heartland of Bengal, among the countries that "gladdened the hearts" of the teachers of the Buddhist Sthaviravada, or School of the Elders. Other countries mentioned include Kashmir in the north, Gandhara (now in Afghanistan and Pakistan) in the west, China in the north and east, and Sri Lanka in the south, suggesting the immensity of the realm of Buddhist culture within which Bengal was included as a major center.

A seventh-century Chinese pilgrim, I-ch'ing, even states that a temple for Chinese Buddhists was established in Bengal under royal patronage in the second century. As this was a time when Buddhism was still in an early phase of establishment in China, this would indicate the international importance of old Bengal as a primary source of the teaching.

In the fifth century C.E., the Chinese traveler Fa-hsien found Buddhism flourishing in Bengal. He reports more than twenty Buddhist establishments in Tamralipti, a major trade center, where he spent two years copying Buddhist scriptures and iconographic art. Archaeologists have discovered numerous examples of Bengali Buddhist statuary and epigraphic records from the fifth and sixth centuries. These artifacts include figures of Maitreya, the Future Buddha, and the bodhisattvas Manjusri and Avalokitesvara, all important images of Mahayana Buddhism. An early sixth-century grant also records the founding of a Mahayana community in Bengal by the great master Shantideva.

The famous seventh-century Chinese pilgrim Hsuan-tsang gives extensive accounts of Buddhist establishments in Bengal, confirming the currency of both Hinayana and Mahayana Buddhism. Hsuan-tsang's own tutor at the great Buddhist university of Nalanda, at that time the head of the monastery, was from a noble Bengali family. Several kings of the Candra dynasty, which ruled in east Bengal from the sixth to the eighth centuries, were also devout Buddhists, and the Buddhist complex at Harikela in east Bengal was a renowned center of learning during this era.

It was largely under the illustrious Pala dynasty (c. 750–1200 CE) that Tantrism emerged as a major movement in old Bengali Buddhism, profoundly influencing the development of Buddhism in Tibet. The Pala dynasty ruled not only Bengal, but at times included parts of Bihar, Assam, and Orissa as well. The famous Buddhist university of Nalanda in Bihar, absorbed into the Bengali political and cultural sphere, reached the height of its glory under Pala rule.

Another major Buddhist complex, Vikramalashila, was founded by Dharmapala (c. 775-810 CE), the second Pala king. With six colleges, one hundred and fourteen teachers, over a hundred temples, and accommodations for three thousand students, Vikramalashila outshone even Nalanda. Large numbers of seekers from Tibet and Nepal, as well as various parts of India, gathered there to study Buddhism.

In the time of the third Pala king, Devapala (810-847 CE), the king of the Shailendra dynasty of Southeast Asia requested (and received) a grant of revenue from five villages to support a monastery at Nalanda. The powerful Shailendra king, who ruled in Java, Sumatra, and Malaya, wanted to establish a center in the Buddhist heartland where students from his own domain could go to study. The magnificent Buddhist monument of Borobodur in central Java was built by the Shailendras, its grand design testifying to the prestige of the Buddhist teaching.

Thus the influence of Buddhism under the patronage of the Bengali Palas extended over a vast area, from Tibet and Nepal to Indonesia. The Sanskrit alphabet used by Kobo Daishi, the founder of Tantric Buddhism in eighth-century Japan, who brought it from China, also clearly points to a Bengali cultural origin, with a recognizable resemblance even to the letters used for modern Bengali and Assamese. At that time there were three major trade routes connecting Bengal with China, including the Tufan-Nepal route through Tibet.

Many important figures of Tibetan tradition were educated in the Bengali Buddhist tradition, and a number of native Bengalis also played important roles in the establishment of Buddhism in Tibet. There are supposed to have been 84 Tantric Siddhas, or adepts, born in Bengal between the 10th and 12th centuries. Perhaps it is not coincidental that this period immediately follows the rise of the Five Houses of classical Zen in China, and coincides with the brilliant Sung dynasty literary articulation of Zen. It also coincides with the rise of Complete Reality Taoism in China, a neo-Taoist movement that resembles both Zen and Tantric Buddhism.

Tantra and Other Religions

Bengali Tantric Buddhism also undoubtedly influenced the development of Shaivite Nathism. Some of the Buddhist Siddhas are also considered Natha Siddhas, illustrating the nondogmatic nature of Tantrism. Tantric Buddhist theory and practice were also adopted by several Vaishnavite sects. Traces of Tantric Buddhism can also be seen in the teachings of famous mystic poet Kabir, as well as in the Sikhism of Guru Nanak. Like some Taoists and Sufis, some of the Tantric Siddhas were also famed as alchemists.

It appears that elements of Bengali Tantric Buddhism may have also been adopted by Sufis from the Islamic tradition.

When the Hindu Sena dynasty supplanted the Palas in Bengal, elitist Brahminical reaction against egalitarian Tantric Buddhist ideas and practices led to suppression of Buddhism. When Turki Muslims subsequently supplanted the Senas, it is said, Buddhists welcomed Islam, which was similarly casteless and egalitarian in spirit, and many formally converted to the new religion.

Ancient cordiality between Muslims and Tantric Buddhists has survived up to the present in Ladakh, "Little Tibet," in spite of recent outside agitation. The Dalai Lama of Tibet has also said that the Tibetan Muslims have kept the best of Tibetan culture.[a]

There were apparently Sufis in Bengal before the Turki ouster of the Hindu Senas. It may not be coincidental that the first Afghan Sufi to use the love motif, so characteristic of Tantric Buddhism, lived in the 11th and 12th centuries, not long after the greatest flourishing of the Bengali Siddhas, in an area where Tantric Buddhism had also been thriving. The illustrious 13th-century Jalaluddin Rumi, known for his love poetry, was originally from Balkh, in Afghanistan. It is well established that there was contact between this region and Buddhist Bengal during the Pala dynasty.

The Chishti order of dervishes, which originated in the 10th century and specialized in the use of music to induce ecstasy, is mentioned in connection with Bengal. The Chishti order was an offshoot of the Sufi Khajagan, whose fourth master, Abdul Khaliq Gujduvani (d. 1190), may have learned the technique of "prayer of the heart," it is thought, from Buddhists of the Hindu Kush who practiced recitation of mantras.[b]

Mantric practice is a characteristic of Tantric Buddhism, and Bengal and the Hindu Kush area are known to have been in contact during the Pala dynasty. Musicians of the Chishti order have been respected for many centuries throughout the Indian subcontinent, where the influence of this order has lasted to the present day.

The Shattari branch of the Naqshbandi order, also descended from the Khajagan, is also mentioned as having been active in Bengal. The Shattaris were known for a rapid method of spiritual illumination; this peculiarity is also associated with certain Zen and Tantric Buddhist teachings, although the methods used are not necessarily the same.[c]

Sufis from the Suhrawardi order, which was founded in the 12th century and employed both ecstatic and quiescent exercises, are also known to have worked in Bengal. Many of them are said to be buried there. Use of ecstasy and quiescence to facilitate subtler perceptions are also characteristic of Tantric Buddhism, as seen in the songs of the Bengali Siddhas.

The modern heirs of the Tantric Siddhas in Bengal are the Bauls, who like their spiritual ancestors are fundamentally nonsectarian, popular, often considered unorthodox like the Tantrists, and also use vernacular songs rather than intellectual dogma to convey their teachings.

Tantric Practice

There are countlessly many forms of Tantric practice, by the nature of its use of the materials of everyday life, including both the inner resources of the mind and body as well as the outer resources of the intellectual, cultural, and material environment. While customary observances of Tantrism, as well as other forms of Buddhism, may at times become locally stereotyped, there remains overall a broad external diversity in every form of Buddhism, including Tantra. Beneath this methodological diversity lies the esoteric unity of the fundamental continuum of Buddhism.

The unity of the continuum of Buddhism is recapitulated within Tantra, just as Hinayana Buddhism is recapitulated with Mahayana Buddhism. Tantra is part of a unified continuum with Hinayana and Mahayana Buddhism, and it also contains and consummates a unified continuum of all three phases of Buddhism within the specifically Tantric mode of expression and practice.

Typical misperceptions of Tantra result from obscuration of this continuum through obsession with the outer forms. When the observer is obsessed with local and temporal forms of any of the stages, be it Hinayana, Mahayana, or Tantric Buddhism, the fundamental unity of the continuum is obscured.

In the context of Tantric Buddhism, the principles of Hinayana and Mahayana Buddhism are personified as supernal beings, or represented by letters or abstract images. The practice are carried out in the process of the individual's mental relationship to this esoteric world. Those who only observe from outside, or those within tradition who have forgotten what they are doing, may see or experience this kind of practice as a form of idolatry, apparently quite different from the religious models of exoteric Buddhism. From a unitarian pan-Buddhist point of view, however, the differences are only external.

This is why there is no religious bigotry in Tantric Buddhism. Recognizing the value of each phase of philosophy and practice in its own proper time in the evolution of the individual and society, the Tantric outlook is able to integrate the whole range of Buddhist teachings and practices. In the same way, the Tantric outlook is able to appreciate and employ teachings and practices of other religions or systems of culture and thought ambient within the host communities and civilizations of the esoteric Buddhist world.

All the ranges of Buddhism, including the various ranges of Tantra, are implicity represented in the practical songs, the *carya-giti,* of the old Bengali Tantric adepts or Siddhas. While it is necessary to defer the greater part of the illustration to commentary on the songs themselves, some sense of the practicalities of the three stages of Buddhism can be gained from comparison of certain basic exercises.

The continuum of the three successive levels of Buddhism might be described as purification, integration, and re-creation.

The first level of Buddhism addresses the problem of mental clarification, dissolving gross attachment to the notional world. The purpose of this type of exercise is to seek insight into objective truth by overcoming the subjective emotional, perceptual, and intellectual biases that are based on ignorant selfishness and cultural conditioning. This is the stage in which personal nirvana is to be realized.

The second level addresses the problem of harmonizing unbiased insight into objective truth with the everyday world of historically conditioned social, intellectual, and perceptual convention. The purpose of this type of exercise is to discover and uncover objective truth everywhere, hidden in ordinary life beneath a veneer of appearances formulated of frozen perceptions. This is the stage in which the nirvanic quintessence of both persons and things is realized.

The third stage finally goes beyond duality in perception of absolute and relative. Everything in relative and imaginary reality reminds the Tantric Buddhist of absolute truth, and this guides the understanding and expression of both material and abstract dimensions of life.

In the first stage, living is a form of responsibility; in the second stage, living is a form of duty; in the third stage, living is a form of artistry, encompassing responsibility and duty in creative devotion. Living in all its many aspects becomes a practical art of expressing a constructive relationship with absolute truth in the context of all life.

Tantra is the consummation of the wedding of absolute and relative knowledge, of insight and compassion. As the simultaneous realization of the transcendence and integration is learned in the first two stages of Buddhism, continuity with Tantra is also reflected in the first two stages, just as the first two stages are also expressed within the total context of Tantra.

In the Hinayana teaching of the Pali *Dhammapada,* Buddha says, "Just as many kinds of garlands can be made from a heap of flowers, so also much good can be done by a mortal being."[1] In the unitarian Mahayana teaching of the hybrid Sanskrit *Saddharmapundarika-sutra,* Buddha says, "All productive activities and means of livelihood are not at variance with the character of reality." Tantric Buddhism is a fully developed manifestation of these realizations. "All forms are forms of Buddha; all sounds are voices of Buddha."

The integrity of the whole range of Buddhism, and its recapitulation in Tantra, can be seen in the symbolism of the pan-Buddhist personification of universal compassion, Avalokitesvara. The name of this personification is sometimes translated "Lord Who Looks Down," or sometimes "Lord Who Regards the Cry of the World." In the West, this figure is best known by the Chinese name Kuan-yin, commonly called the Goddess of Mercy. The impersonal meaning of the name is "capacity of objective observation."

All pan-Buddhists and Tantrists meditate on Avalokitesvara at some time. The integration of Buddhist enlightenment with the world, and the intrinsic unity of Buddhism underlying a diverse range of method that encompasses other religions as well, is poetically explained in the description of the teaching of the bodhisattva Avalokitesvara found in the unitarian *Avatamsakasutra* or *Flower Ornament Scripture.*

> I know a way of enlightening practice called "undertaking great compassion without delay," which sets about impartially guiding all sentient beings to perfection, dedicated to protecting and guiding sentient beings by communicating knowledge to them through all media.
>
> Established in this method of enlightening practice undertaking great compassion without delay, I appear in the midst of the activities of all sentient beings without leaving the presence of all Buddhas, and take care of them by means of generosity, kind speech, beneficial actions, and cooperation. I also develop sentient beings by appearing in various forms. I gladden and develop them by purity of vision of inconceivable forms radiating auras of light, and I take care of them and develop them by speaking to them according to their mentalities, and by showing conduct according to their inclinations, and by magically producing various forms and teaching them doctrines commensurate with their various interests, and by inspiring them to begin to accumulate good qualities, by showing them projections according to their mentalities, by appearing to them as members of their own various races and conditions, and by living together with them.[2]

The syncretism attributed to Tantric Buddhism is a result of application of these principles. It cannot be considered in itself a degeneration, as ultraconservative sectarians and externalist scholars have ordinarily considered it. There is the possibility of degeneration in the practice of each and every phase of Buddhism, not only Tantra. Buddhist texts, both Hinayana and Mahayana, are often explicit on this point.

There are different characteristic deteriorations of each of the three phases of Buddhism, but in spite of their differences in expression, they are fundamentally based on the same set of weaknesses of human psychology. Ignorance or nihilism may take the form of extreme quietism on the level of Hinayana Buddhism, whereas it may take the form of decadence on the level of Mahayana Buddhism or adventurism on the level of Tantric Buddhism. Greed may manifest itself as vanity on one level, officiousness on another level, and ambitiousness on a third level. Aggression may appear in the form of prudishness, in the form of proselytism, or in the form of authoritarianism; or in a combination of all three of these forms.

The deteriorations of religious forms consequent upon approaching them with greed, aggression, and ignorance are not limited to Tantric Buddhism, or to any particular religion.

Tantra and Sexuality

Apart from idolatry and hybridization of various kinds attributed to Tantric Buddhism, the most commonly assailed feature of this form of Buddhism is the conscious transformation of sexuality into religious experience. Although this aspect of Tantric Buddhism is no different from any other form of Buddhism in being susceptible to misunderstanding, misuse and degeneration, that is a different matter from saying that it is inherently degenerate. The latter opinion is more a reflection of the mentality of those who hold it, or of external misperception, than it is of the Tantric art of love.

It is an unfortunate fact, nonetheless, that the name of Tantra has been used to conjure up images of promiscuous orgies. Exaggerations and degenerations aside, such images appear to be derived in the main from Brahmanical paranoias about race and caste mixing.

The natural ecstasy of Tantric Buddhist love is of an entirely different qualitative range than that of ordinary sexual feeling. It is incomparably more refined, and more subtly ecstatic, leaving a more stable impression on the quality of life, resulting in a more permanent mental enhancement, than the temporary satisfaction of ordinary sensuality. For some, in fact, it is a purely psychic or spiritual practice, without a physical counterpart; and for some it is purely symbolic, representing a metaphysical experience.

The esoteric significance of sexual union in Buddhism, and also the invisibility of this level of understanding and experience to the vulgar eye, are explained at some length in the final book of the pan-Buddhist *Flower Ornament Scripture,* in the story of the visit of the pilgrim Sudhana, "Wealth of Good," to the woman Vasumitra, "Friend of the World."

According to the story, the pilgrim is directed to Vasumitra in the course of a long journey to call on spiritual benefactors. Vasumitra is not a sectarian Buddhist, but a devotee of the god of light. The pilgrim is sent to her, however, by a Buddhist nun, who is further described as having attained an enlightening liberation characterized by removal of all vain imaginings. This manner of setting up the visit illustrates the sense of order in Buddhist practice, the need for purification and clarification before integration and re-creation.

According to the Buddhist nun, Vasumitra lives in a city called Ratnavyuha, "Array of Jewels," in a country called Durga, "Difficult to Approach." These details illustrate both the promise and the perils of this level of experience.

When the pilgrim had made his way to the place where Vasumitra lived, people tried to discourage him from visiting her. This illustrates the superficial mind focused only on external forms. According to the story in the scripture, the people who tried to dissuade the pilgrim from visiting the woman were those "who did not know of Vasumitra's virtues or the scope of her knowledge." They said to Sudhana, "What has someone like you—with senses so calm and subdued, so aware, so clear, without confusion or distraction, your gaze focused discreetly right before you, your mind not overwhelmed by sensations, not clinging to appearances, your eyes averted from involvement in all forms, your mind so cool and steady, your way of life profound, wise, oceanic, your mind free from agitation or despondency—what have you to do with Vasumitra?"

This passage underscores Sudhana's level of preparation before visiting Vasumitra, as well as the appearance of incongruity to those who do not perceive the integrity of Vasumitra or the possibility of Sudhana's reintegration.

There were others, however, who in fact "knew the excellence of the virtues of Vasumitra, and were aware of the scope of her knowledge." These people encouraged the pilgrim

Sudhana and gave him precise directions, adding, "You have really made a gain if you ask about Vasumitra. You surely seek Buddhahood; you surely want to make yourself a refuge for all sentient beings; you surely want to transform the notion of purity."

This passage represents awareness of a higher level of purity, in the world but not stained by worldly vanities. The esoteric aspect of this level of Buddhism is not necessarily a matter of secrecy, as the story illustrates, but an issue of perception and knowledge. The spiritual eye sees what the mundane eye does not.

When the pilgrim finally meets Vasumitra, he finds that she is not only physically beautiful, but that she also "was well versed in all arts and sciences," she had "learned to use the magic of true knowledge," and she had "mastered all aspects of the expedient means of enlightening beings." The image is not one of a sexual temptress, but of a paragon of enlightening integration of the absolute and the relative.

Finally, in conversation with the pilgrim, Vasumitra reveals the secrets of spirituality in intimate union. "I have attained an enlightening liberation called 'ultimately dispassionate,'" she says, explaining the means and end of her universal adaptation; "To gods, in accord with their inclinations and interests, I appear in the form of a goddess of surpassing splendor and perfection; and to all other types of beings I accordingly appear in the form of a female of their species, of surpassing splendor and perfection. And all who come to me with minds full of passion, I teach them so that they become free of passion. Those who have heard my teaching and attain dispassion achieve an enlightening concentration called 'realm of nonattachment.'"

This is a degree of profound satisfaction and spiritual transport unattainable by mundane emotions and gross sensuality. Vasumitra goes on to explain, "Some attain dispassion as soon as they see me, and achieve an enlightening concentration called 'delight in joy.'

"Some attain dispassion merely by talking with me, and achieve an enlightening concentration called 'treasury of unimpeded sound.'

"Some attain dispassion just by holding my hand, and achieve an enlightening concentration called 'basis of going to all buddha-lands.'

"Some attain dispassion just by staying with me, and achieve an enlightening concentration called 'light of freedom from bondage.'

"Some attain dispassion just by gazing at me, and achieve an enlightening concentration called 'tranquil expression.'

"Some attain dispassion just by embracing me, and achieve an enlightening concentration called 'womb receiving all sentient beings without rejection.'

"Some attain dispassion just by kissing me, and achieve an enlightening concentration called 'contact with the treasury of virtue of all beings.'

"All those who come to me I establish in this enlightening liberation of ultimate dispassion, on the brink of the stage of unimpeded all-knowledge."[3]

Vasumitra finally explains that she was inspired to seek supreme perfect enlightenment by Manjusri, the supernal bodhisattva who represents both wisdom and knowledge, transcendental insight into emptiness, as well as formal mastery of art and science.

Thus, the scriptural story illustrates the principles of both the theory and practice of Tantra, showing how this manifestation of Buddhism may be externally controversial because of the different perceptions of observers, while inwardly coherent as an expression of fully integrated Buddhist spirituality.

Songs of the Adepts

The Tantric songs of the old Bengali adepts translated here are thought to date from the 10th and 11th centuries. This collection is currently believed to be the only full length text in the Old Bengali language extant. In translating it from the original Old Bengali, I have made use of Nilratan Sen's critical edition of *Caryagitikos,* which includes a late Sanskrit commentary in Bengali script by Munidatta, thought to be of the 15th century; and Tarapad Mukhopadhyay's critical edition in his study *Old Bengali Language and Text.* The translator's commentaries are intended to expound the meanings of the songs, which are often in symbolic "twilight language," in the overall context of pan-Buddhism, specifically to illustrate the continuity of Tantra with other forms of Buddhism.[4]

1

LUI

The body is a tree, with five branches;
When the mind is unstable, time enters in.
Firmly determine the Greater Bliss;
Ask the Teacher, says Lui, and know!
What is the use of meditation at all?
One dies bound to pleasure and pain.
Give up the bondage of desire,
the hope for keenness of sense;
Draw the wings of emptiness close to your sides.
Lui says, "I am seen in meditation,
Seated on the seat of inhalexhalation."

The body is a tree, with five branches;
When the mind is unstable, time enters in.

The image of the body as a tree is elaborated by the Chinese Zen Buddhist Lan-hsi in his *Treatise on Meditation:* "Ordinary people are like trees: putting the manure of greed and lust on the thin soil of folly and delusion, planting seeds of ignorance, transplanting shoots of form, feeling, perception, conditioning, and consciousness, producing buds of active habit-ridden consciousness, growing roots of attachment and stems of flattery and deceit, sprouting leaves of jealousy and envy, creating trees of affliction, causing flowers of infatuation to bloom, forming fruits of greed, aggression, and ignorance."[5]

In Lui's verse, the "five branches" of the tree of the body may be taken to stand for the limbs and head; or they may be understood to refer to the "five clusters" of form, feeling, perception, conditioning, and consciousness, which are commonly used in Buddhist literature to represent a mortal being, as also in Lan-hsi's essay. "When the mind is unstable, time enters in" because the body is governed by the mind and is therefore affected, even afflicted, by fluctuations in the mind, which bring the whole being under the sway of time.

Aristotle is reported to have said, "The soul is not within the body; rather the body is within the soul, because the soul is more extensive than the body, and greater in magnitude."[6] Were the term "mind" in the Buddhist sense substituted for Aristotle's "soul," this statement could have come from India, in explanation of the primary Buddhist emphasis on care and cultivation of mind. The philosophers and physicians of Taoism, which is much like Tantric Buddhism, also regard instability and hyperactivity of the mind to be direct causes of physical unwellness and deterioriation.

Firmly determine the Greater Bliss;
Ask the Teacher, says Lui, and know!

The Greater Bliss is subtle transport, beyond the ordinary senses of joy and sorrow. Although it is a natural phenomenon, this is nevertheless sporadic in people subject to ordinary social and psychological conditioning. Therefore it is not accessible as a constant resource unless and until it is deliberately stabilized. This is why there is, in the stage of ultimate realization, no contradiction between natural and attained enlightenment.

"Ask the Teacher, says Lui, and know." This simple exhortation contains many meanings. On the surface is the sense of the need for guidance. In practice it is necessary to "ask the teacher" in order to know, because the confused or unenlightened mind cannot guide itself to enlightenment. Underlying this is the sense of what "teacherhood" is all about. It is properly for the sake of enlightening knowledge alone that one goes to a teacher; not for imagined blessings or graces, let alone lesser goals.

The emphasis on knowing highlights the necessity of direct, firsthand personal experience on the way to enlightenment. The aim is not to be rescued, to be saved, to be convinced, to be converted, to be forgiven, to be absolved, to believe, to have faith, but to *know*. It is through this knowledge, this personal experience of the spiritual euphoria of enlightenment, that one can attain salvation, certainty, and serenity.

What is the use of meditation at all?
One dies bound to pleasure and pain.

After Prince Siddhartha gave up his royal inheritance to seek permanent peace of mind, he followed two Hindu yoga teachers. The first one taught him to reach several stages of meditation, in the highest of which there is no longer any pain or pleasure. The second one taught him to reach a series of stages of abstraction, the most refined being described as neither perception nor nonperception.

Siddhartha found that these yogic experiences seemed to last for very long periods of time, in subjective terms. Yet they inevitably dissolved, leaving the seeker back in the world, now with a profound longing and sorrow at the loss of celestial states. Thus it was that Siddhartha came to realize that these practices and experiences were not eternal spirituality itself, but rather temporal methods of cultivating different perspectives. Siddartha's subsequent detachment from all mental states, both ordinary and extraordinary, ultimately led to his liberation.

This point was later reemphasized in Zen Buddhism, to remedy centuries of devolutionary sectarian cultism dependent upon attachment to limited theories, practices, and altered states of mind. The Tantric adept Lui here expresses the same stage, known in Universalist Buddhism as "abandoning the raft," or letting go of the means when the end has been realized.

In the idea that meditation is a means, not an end, is implicitly echoed the principle that to enter into meditation practice in the wrong frame of mind is useless and even harmful. Seeking personal power, or thrilling experiences, or self-deceptive reality-avoidance, or obsessiveness in general, are unsuitable bases for meditation. Lui warns people not to become wrongly attached to meditation; he also reminds people to scrutinize their own motives and actions. Seekers need to ask themselves what they are really thinking of meditating for in the first place.

Give up the bondage of desire,
the hope for keenness of sense;
Draw the wings of emptiness close to your sides.

Desire is part of our inherited instinctive constitution, as a mechanism of survival and evolution. Desire can also be influenced and cultivated beyond survival value by habit and conditioning. Bondage to desire, preoccupation with craving for intense experience, makes the individual and community especially vulnerable to exaggerated selfishness, aggression, heedlessness, and short-sightedness.

To give up the bondage of desire is to be able to experience and understand desire without compulsiveness, without augmentation of craving. This is a way to be more objective about desire, and therefore less under the control of associated feelings such as hope, fear, elation, and disappointment.

Ironically, perhaps, attempts to control desire may in fact have the reverse effect of magnifying desire in the mind of someone deliberately trying to control it. This is why Buddhists resort to perception of "emptiness" to transcend the bondage of desire without laboring to extinguish desire itself.

By viewing desire and its objects as conditional, emphemeral phenomena, and viewing repetitious thinking about desire as self-delusion, Buddhists "draw the wings of emptiness close to their sides," transcending the bondage of desire even in the very midst of desire.

To those already obsessed with desire and its fulfillment and frustration, this way of managing desire can seem negative or nihilistic. When the mind is already set on its own preoccupations in that way, the felicitous outcome on the "other side" of liberation from obsession is not even thinkable. The Buddhist goal of realizing emptiness is actually a better happiness, as illustated in the ancient *Dhammapada.* Buddha himself presents the pattern of spiritual regeneration following upon mortification or transcendence of the lower self: "Do not indulge in negligence, do not be intimate with attachment to desire. The vigilant one, meditative, gains great happiness."[7]

Lui says, "I am seen in meditation,
Seated on the seat of inhalexhalation."

This verse may seem, at a glance, to contradict the earlier verse questioning the use of meditation. It must be realized, however, that the earlier verse defines the realizations upon which wholesome meditation and lucid vigilance can be practiced.

The term "inhalexhalation" is a coinage intended to imitate the original technical expression, underlining the sense of the breathing as one continuous cycle in two phases. This is considered a useful exercise for concentrating a scattered mind and preparing it to perceive reality more objectively.

In ancient Buddhism, mindfulness of breathing and mindfulness of impermanence were referred to as two *amrtadvara* or "doors of immortality" leading to nirvana, or clearing of the mind. Mindfulness of breathing was considered the better door in the sense that by nature it contains the other door within it.

The Indian meditation master Prajnatara spoke of both application and realization of this practice in these terms, five hundred years before Lui: "Breathing in, I do not dwell on the elements of mind or body; breathing out, I do not get involved in myriad things."

Zen Buddhists of the Far East, whose teachings resemble those of these Vajrayana Siddhacaryas of Bengal, consider Prajnatara (fifth century C.E.) their twenty-seventh Indian patriarch. Chinese records say he was from "Eastern India," which would include the area of what had been Magadha when Buddha was born there a thousand years before Prajnatara, and the Bengali Paia dynasty when Lui sang there five or six hundred years later. Buddha's mother-tongue, Magadhi, and Lui's "Old Bengali" language are directly related.

Thus it is possible to see, in more than one dimension, the historical continuity of Buddhism in its first homeland over a period of at least fifteen hundred years, unbroken through what conventional scholarship generally designates Hinayana, Mahayana, and Vajrayana Buddhism.

2

KUKKURI

Having milked the turtle, the pitcher holds no more;
The crocodile eats the tree's tamarind.
Listen to the courtyard being swept, O mistress;
A thief has stolen the earrings
in the middle of the night.
Father-in-law gone to sleep, the bride is awake;
The earrings have been taken by a thief—
where does one go to look for them?
By day, the bride is scared of the crows;
When scared at night, she goes to Kamarupa.
Kukkuri sings of such practice:
It enters the heart of one in a million.

Having milked the turtle, the pitcher holds no more;
The crocodile eats the tree's tamarind.

The turtle that withdraws its head and limbs and shuts itself up in its shell for safety was anciently used as an image of the practice of withdrawal of the senses from external stimulation. Sometimes this is used for stress reduction, for mental and physical health. Sometimes the practice is applied to the effort to recollect a scattered mind, or to abstract processes of thoughts and judgment from the influence of immediate stimuli.

When withdrawal is overused, or indulged in for escapist purposes, the results are stultifying rather than restorative. The first line of this couplet expresses this by saying, in effect, that there is a limit to which the "turtle" exercise can be optimally employed ("milk" also means "utilize" in Old Bengali, much as it can mean "exploit" in modern English).

The crocodile is the picture of ferocity, the tamarind a leguminous tree with a pulpy fruit. This presents a counterpoint to the passivity of withdrawal, actively sinking one's teeth into the knotty problems of real life. A Zen proverb says, "The level field of equanimity is littered with the skulls of the dead; it is only the experts who can get through the forest of thorny problems."

Listen to the courtyard being swept, O mistress;
A thief has stolen the earrings
in the middle of the night.

The mistress is formless insight, listening is attention. The courtyard being swept is the spontaneous passing away of random thoughts and feelings.

The first line represents a concrete exercise in clearing the mind of inward chatter. The thief is natural bliss, or the bliss of naturalness (sahajananda); the earrings are artificialities. The middle of the night is formless, silent mental equipoise. The second line describes the exercise taking effect.

Father-in-law gone to sleep, the bride is awake;
The earrings have been taken by a thief—
where does one go to look for them?

The father-in law stands for conventionally structured thinking, bound by rules of conditioned habit that are ultimately arbitrary yet rigidly maintained. The bride stands for nondiscursive insight, seeing immediately and directly, thus always fresh and new.

When the "father- in-law" of authoritarian conventional thinking has "gone to sleep" in the quiescence of cessational meditation, then the "bride" of nonconceptual knowing can "waken" and operate without interference in observational meditation.

When acquired superficialities have been dropped through the experience of naturalness ("the earrings have been taken by a thief"), there is no obstacle to looking back into the mystery of the essence and source of consciousness ("where does one go to look?").

By day, the bride is scared of the crows;
When scared at night, she goes to Kamarupa.

Daytime stands for the world of differences. Silent, formless insight is "drowned out" by the clamor of the worldly mind, with its internal bantering and chattering, whose crude stimulation distracts and dulls the faculty of finer sense.

Night stands for nirvana, or the experience of the absolute. Kamarupa, a place name that literally means "Form of Desire," stands for a locus on the subtle energy body, and spiritual bliss.

When experience of the absolute in nirvanic quiescence goes so deep as to put one in danger of slipping into complete annihilation, the subtle awareness of formless insight maintains the "ember" of life in the medium of spiritual ecstasy.

This is the meaning of the classic Zen verse that says, "It shines right at midnight, and does not appear at dawn."

Kukkuri sings of such practice:
It enters the heart of one in a million.

The Siddha concludes by reminding his hearers that what he is singing of is a practical process, not just philosophical or literary conceits. Bodhidharma, the founder of Zen, said, "There are many who see the Way; there are few who practice it." The *Flower Ornament Scripture,* a root source of Far Eastern Tantric Buddhism, emphasizes this point strongly:

Like a person skilled in medicine
who cannot cure his own disease:
so are those who .are learned
but do not apply the teaching.
Like someone counting others' treasures
without half a coin of his own:
so is the one who is learned
who does not practice the teaching.
Like one who is born in a royal palace
yet freezes and starves,
so are those who are learned
but do not practice the teaching.[8]

3

VIRUBA

A single wine-making woman enters two houses;
Using fermenting agents, she makes the wine.
In natural calm, she makes the wine;
Who ages not nor dies is firm of body and mind.
Seeing the sign on the tenth door,
The buyer came of his own accord.
Sixty-four pitchers are given in display;
Once a customer's gone in, there's no coming out.
One small container, with a slender tube;
Viruba says, "Make movements calmly."

A single wine-making woman enters two houses;
Using fermenting agents, she makes the wine.

The wine-making woman is wisdom, the two houses are samsara and nirvana. Samsara is the mundane world, and nirvana is absolute truth, or transcendent inner peace. The fermenting agents are developmental practices, the wine-making is the process of awakening, and the wine is the spiritual euphoria of realization.

According to the *Flower Ornament Scripture* a bodhisattva, who is someone in the process of enlightening self and others, has both a face of nirvana and a face of samsara. The insight of Buddhas penetrates both the relative and the absolute, producing two kinds of knowledge. Thus "the winemaking woman enters two houses" and "makes the wine."

In natural calm, she makes the wine;
Who ages not nor dies is firm of body and mind.

Insight has to be stabilized before it can be employed constructively. A classical Zen Buddhist image for this is the flame and glass of a lamp. The flame is like insight, the glass is like calmness; without stable calmness, access to insight fluctuates like an unsheltered candle in the wind.

"Who ages not nor dies" is the Buddha-nature, which is believed to be the natural and inherent essence of living beings.

T'ien-t'ai and Hua-yen Buddhism also call this "mind in its aspect of suchness" in contrast to "mind in its aspect of repetitious arousal." In Taoist hygiene theory, which has close affinities to Tantric Buddhism, detachment from fluctuations of thought and feeling in favor of calm immersion in the essence of mind itself is considered a restorative "elixir" that reduces both physical and mental stress, thus fostering health and longer life.

Seeing the sign on the tenth door,
The buyer came of his own accord.

According to Munidatta's commentary, the "tenth door" is the "door of Vairocana," who is the Adi-Buddha, or primordial Buddha, the essence and function of cosmic consciousness represented by the sun and its rays of light. The *Flower Ornament Scripture* features the "Tower of Vairocana," containing infinite infinities within it, symbolizing the awakening of the whole mind.

Munidatta comments that "seeing the sign on the tenth door" means "seeing the sign of great joy, pleasure, and delight," which corresponds to the experience of the first of the ten stages of enlightenment expounded by the comprehensive *Flower Ornament Scripture,* in which one begins to rise above mundane entanglements by means of the intensity of joy in contemplating the realization of Buddhahood.

Absorbed into the life attitude, the experience of spiritual joy at the thought of enlightenment, leads one naturally and spontaneously into the path of refinement. Thus Viruba sings that the "buyer," that is, the spiritual speeker, "came of his own accord."

Sixty-four pitchers are given in display;
Once a customer's gone in, there's no coming out.

According to convention, worldly arts and sciences are traditionally said to be sixty-four in number. "Sixty-four pitchers" may be taken to refer to the sum total of worldly knowledge. These are "given in display" in the sense that things of the world are not permanently there, only temporarily.

Once we are born in the world, we inevitably die; "there's no coming out" alive. Any aspect of the world or worldly knowledge could become a dead-end obsession, for anyone who remained heedless of the transitory and mutable nature of mundane phenomena.

One small container, with a slender tube;
Viruba says, "Make movements calmly."

The small container with a slender tube is the human body, with focus on the respiratory system. As explained earlier, mindfulness of breathing is a traditional method of cultivating concentration and calmness. This helps the individual to live in the world constructively without being unduly influenced by external pressure and confusion.

The quality of the breathing is taken as a barometer of mental state. Rapid, shallow breathing, for example, would be expected to coincide with some sort of mental agitation, whereas slow, deeper breathing would be expected to coincide with calmness. Therefore, while the breathing slows as the mind slows, conversely the mind can also be calmed by breathing more calmly.

Thus, while the last line of the verse can be taken as a general recommendation to balance activity with calmness, it is also a specific direction for mindful breathing. In practice, these two meanings reinforce one another, and ultimately coincide.

In more advanced meditation, the "slender tube" can also be understood to mean the "central channel" visualized along the course of the spinal cord of the physical body. The "movements" of opening, energizing, and clearing the channel in meditation must be made with great care. Generally speaking, this is only possible after the mind-breath continuum is already calmed.

4

GUNTARI

Pressing the three channels,
the yogini gives an embrace:
Lotus and lightning mix together in the afternoon.
Yogini, I cannot live a moment without you;
Kissing your face, I sip the lotus sweet juice.
After casting off, the yogini is no longer affected;
Leaving the source of mind, she's soared to ecstasy.
The key has been turned in the lock
of the passage of breath;
The moon and the sun spread their wings.
Guntari says, "I am strong in making love;
A man inside a woman, perpetually erect."

Pressing the three channels,
the yogini gives an embrace:
Lotus and lightning mix together in the afternoon.

In Tantric yoga, the body is visualized as consisting of a network of energy channels and concentration points. This exercise facilitates transcendence of the physical body while retaining creative capacity, without lapsing into nihilistic indifference.

The "three channels" are the right, left, and center channels, forming the main trunk of this network. The right and left channels are called channels of perception and dalliance, the central channel is called the channel of purification. One form of inner exercise involves mentally circulating the experiences fostered in the channels of perception and dalliance into the channel of purification, where they are clarified and resolved.

According to Munidatta, the yogini (female yogi) symbolizes *nairatmya* or selflessness, and the pressing of the three channels by the embrace of the yogini means making them free of manifestation. Selflessness means relativity, in Buddhist terms, in the sense that nothing that can be apprehended exists in and of itself. This realization is the ultimate "clearing" of the energy channels, whose existence is relative to the mind, visualized as actual in order to counteract the grossness of ordinary bodily sense.

Lotus and lightning symbolize insight and skill in means, which are the two major complementary pragmatic facets of enlightenment. These two "wings" of Buddhism are also represented by female and male. Sexual intercourse symbolizes the perfect harmonization of intuitive insight into the essential nature of ultimate reality with practical knowledge of the characteristics of mundane actualities.

The afternoon represents the combining of light and darkness, which symbolizes the integration of perceptions of relative and absolute realities, and the discursive and nondiscursive cognitions that take place through these experiences. Thus the "afternoon" is the proper "time" of the "mixing" of the "lotus and lightning."

Yogini, I cannot live a moment without you;
Kissing your face, I sip the lotus sweet juice.

The ancient Chinese *Tao Te Ching* says. "When people are born they are supple, and when they die they are stiff. When trees are born they are tender, and when they die they are brittle. Stiffness is thus a companion of death, flexibility is a companion of life."[9]

In Buddhist terms, the selflessness, or emptiness, of all things is expressed and realized as fluidity; nothing is static, everything is an evolving process. Were this not so, everything would come to a standstill, and there would be no room for expression of creative energy.

Kissing the face of the yogini means personally experiencing liberation from views by realizing their relativity to mental states that are themselves relative. The lotus sweet juice is the elixir of immortality, another name for nirvana, or cessation of confusion.

After casting off, the yogini is no longer affected;
Leaving the source of mind, she's soared to ecstasy.

Here Munidatta further defines the yogini as "the yogini of selflessness, representing the thought of enlightenment." After "casting off" entanglement, consciousness is fluid but no longer under the influence of externals.

This nonattachment does not mean remaining stagnant, insensitive, or inactive. Outwardly unburdened by things, inwardly not clinging to stillness, from stillness the thought of enlightenment rises in spiritual transport.

The Chinese Zen master Lin-chi said, "I do not grasp the ordinary or the holy outside, and I do not dwell on the fundamental inside; I see all the way through, and no longer experience confusion."

The key has been turned in the lock
of the passage of breath;
The moon and the sun spread their wings.

As mentioned earlier, the practice of mindfulness of breathing is one of the two "doors to immortality" or gateways to nirvana, including within it the other "door," which is mindfulness of impermanence.

The moon and the sun stand for two kinds of *bodhicitta* or "thought of enlightenment," the fundamental inspiration of Buddhism. The moon represents the *samvrti-bodhicitta* or worldly thought of enlightenment, and the sun represents the *paramartha-bodhicitta* or absolute thought of enlightenment. The worldly thought of enlightenment is based on consciousness of impermanence and conditionality, while the absolute thought of enlightenment is based on direct sensing of the transcendent peace of nirvana.

Thus the couplet says, in effect, that both ordinary thought of enlightenment and transcendent thought of enlightenment are activated through the practice of mindfulness of breathing, when the stage of unobstruction is reached.

This couplet provides pragmatic directions for attaining the state of mind represented by the embrace of the yogini and the intercourse of lotus and lightning.

Guntari says, "I am strong in making love;
A man inside a woman, perpetually erect."

Making love symbolizes the uniting of mystical insight with temporal knowledge and action. The "man" represents *upaya,* expedient means, and the "woman" represents *prajna,* deep insight, or *sunyata,* emptiness or absoluteness.

The "man inside a woman" illustrates the practical principle that expedient means in the true Buddhist sense operate only within the scope of authentic insight. This image also illustrates the metaphysical principle underlying expediency of action, that ways and means are conditional and temporary, thus empty of inherent ultimacy or absoluteness.

That the man is, nonetheless, "perpetually erect" signifies that "emptiness" does not mean nothingness. It is precisely in the fluidity of true emptiness that the creativity of acting on the thought of enlightenment comes to life.

5

CATILA

The flow of existence is impenetrably deep,
its current is swift;
Both banks are muddy,
the middle can't be fathomed.
Catila builds a bridge for the sake of Truth;
People going to the Other Side cross over in safety.
The tree of illusion's cut asunder,
then the pieces joined;
The strong axe of nonduality
is fashioned in nirvana.
Climbing the bridge, go neither right nor left;
Enlightenment is close, not far away.
Any of you people who would go across,
Ask Catila, the unsurpassed master.

The flow of existence is impenetrably deep,
its current is swift;
Both banks are muddy,
the middle can't be fathomed.

As we are swept along by the current of events, we don't really know why; we are constantly occupied with response and adaptation to ever-changing circumstances. We do not know where we came from to begin with, and we do not know where we will go when we perish from this earth; when we try to grasp the origin or the ending of our sense of self, we find they slip from the grip of our perception. And when we try to fathom the process of life in the meanwhile, life in all its possibilities and potentials for better and for worse, we find that it is beyond the power of our conception to fully comprehend.

The way of looking at the human situation illustrated in this couplet is an ordinary method of cultivating the *bodhicitta* or thought of enlightenment. It is not that Buddhism is a pessimistic philosophy, even at the elementary level, as has sometimes been concluded on the basis of fragmentary observation. This type of exercise is not abstract philosophy, but a process of considering the difficulties of our predicament in a broad yet concentrated manner, in order to stimulate our superlative adaptive capacity to develop ourselves even beyond the needs of the immediate conditions.

This "liberation" is not just for personal enjoyment or fulfillment, according to Buddhist philosophy, but for freeing energy and intelligence from short-term individual survival to longterm, far-reaching needs of humanity, our fellow beings, and our environment as a whole.

In Taoist spiritual alchemy, the individual development is referred to as taking over the process of creative evolution, and its reinvestment in the welfare of the world is called partnership in the process of creative evolution.

Catila builds a bridge for the sake of Truth;
People going to the Other Side cross over in safety.

The use of a bridge to symbolize the Buddhist teaching is also common in China and the Far East. The mundane world and conventional reality is called "this side" or "this shore" and transcendence, nirvana, and ultimate t ruth is called the "other side" or the "farther shore."

The adept says that he "builds" this bridge, underscoring the principle that a way across is a temporal expedient, a conditional construction.

The purpose of the bridge is not to get people out of the world, but to conduct them to a completely different perspective on the world. Because of the pliability of consciousness, outside the force-field of conventional usage it is exposed to incalculable dangers from the influences of the environment and the psychological residua in subconscious storage. The bridge is constructed so as to enable people to arrive at transcendence in safety, not swept away by the forcefulness of powerful emotions, ecstatic visions, or other extraordinary experiences occurring to the consciousness no longer defended by the boundaries of customary views.

The tree of illusion's cut asunder,
then the pieces joined;
The strong axe of nonduality
is fashioned in nirvana.

The total path of Buddhism does not end at transcendence of the world, but includes reintegration. The Chinese Zen master Pai-chang said, "A Buddha is just someone who leaves bondage, then comes back within bondage to be a Buddha for others."

In terms of Buddhist Yoga, phenomena have three natures: absolute, relative, and conceptual. The nature of things as conceived *(parikalpita)* is the subjective description projected on things; this is the root and substance of illusion.

To cut the tree of illusion asunder means distinguishing the conceptual nature of things from the relative and absolute natures of things, realizing the unreality of mere description, and letting go the mental grasp on the images of the conceptual description to "see through" to the absolute.

This discerning transcendence of illusion, however, is not the end of the Buddhist path; as the present couplet ilustrates. After having "cut the tree of illusion asunder," then one "rejoins the pieces." By cutting through the illusion that description is itself reality, the practitioner acquires the freedom to operate constructively within the realm of convention, no longer bound by the limits of conditioned thought.

This is the meaning of the nonduality of samsara and nirvana, which is the basis of Universalist and Tantric Buddhism. This nonduality is inaccessible, however, to the mind still enmeshed in its own conceptual descriptions. Only in the inner silence of nirvana is it possible to directly experience nonduality. Zen proverb says, "Let go both hands over a cliff; after dying completely, come back to life; then nothing can deceive you."

Climbing the bridge, go neither right nor left;
Enlightenment is close, not far away.

Using the esoteric imagery of the energy channels to interpret "right" and "left," the first line of this couplet warns the practitioner not to linger in perception or dalliance on the way over. Extraordinary perceptions and experiences may occur as the mind goes beyond the bounds of conventional conditioning. Enthusiasts may become fascinated by these phenomena, thus losing the way to real freedom and enlightenment. Therefore this kind of warning is normal in Buddhist meditation lore.

One of the lures of extraordinary perceptions and experiences is the sense of enhancement, which gives rise to the notion of enlightenment as an accumulation of such attainments. This results in a kind of disorientation that obstructs realization of penetrating insight into the essential. Thus it is said that enlightenment is not far away, in the sense that insight is not something acquired from outside. The Japanese Zen master Dogen wrote, "Why abandon a seat in your own house to idly roam in the dusty realms of alien countries?"

Any of you people who would go across,
Ask Catila, the unsurpassed master.

The bridge stands for method, liberative techniques by which the human mind is freed from arbitrary limitations. Such bridges are constructed by people who have already made the crossing, based on their consequent knowledge of the goal and their subsequent use of available materials to construct means for others to cross over. In order to use a particular method, it is therefore necessary to follow directions, that is, to follow it correctly, in accordance with its expert design.

6

BHUSUKU

Of what is taken and discarded, what remains?
Encircled by clamor,
he scatters to the four quarters.
Its own flesh is the deer's enemy;
Bhusuku the hunter will not let it go for a moment.
The deer neither touches grass nor drinks water;
The deer doesn't know the doe's abode.
The doe speaks, the deer listens: "You, deer!
Abandon this forest and be a wanderer."
As it sprints away,
the hooves of the deer cannot be seen;
Bhusuku says so, but it enters not the ignorant mind.

Of what is taken and discarded, what remains?
Encircled by clamor,
he scatters to the four quarters.

What is taken and discarded is the mortal body. This first line represents contemplation of impermanence. The Japanese Zen master Dogen taught, "If you would be free of greed, first you must leave selfishness behind. In order to leave selfishness behind, the contemplation of impermanence is the foremost mental discipline."

The encircling clamor is the continual fluctuation of the environment, including the ups and downs of fortune and the vagaries of human behavior. Scattering to the four directions means freeing the mind from this knot of anxiety by dissolving the feeling of subject versus object and realizing the ungraspability of things in themselves.

Its own flesh is the deer's enemy;
Bhusuku the hunter will not let it go for a moment.

Desires of the flesh can lead people to unreasonable actions with undesirable consequences. Habitual desires can bind people into limited and limiting routines of behavior. Unchecked by reason, obsession with personal desires is potentially self destructive. In the *Dhammapada,* Buddha says, "Whoever overcomes this clinging vulgar craving in the world, so hard to get over, has sorrows fall away, like drops of water from a lotus."[10]

The hunter is the inner observer, watching for heedless obsessiveness, ready to shoot it down wherever it is found. This represents self-watching, a basic Buddhist exercise. Through the practice of self-watching, one comes to understand how much energy one spends on vanity and futility. This realization can then be used to cultivate a capacity of conscious inner self-regulation.

The deer neither touches grass nor drinks water;
The deer doesn't know the doe's abode.

The deer refraining from fodder and water represents the mind turning away from involvement in habitual routine attachments, which obstruct direct realization of objective truth. The deer not knowing where the doe abides symbolizes the inability of the ordinary conditioned senses and culturally formulated intelligence to know emptiness. The *Sandhinirmocana-sutra* says, "Someone in ignorance who clings to the signs of the world because of overwhelming interest in perceptual and cognitive signs thus cannot think of, or assess, or believe in the ultimate nirvana that obliterates all signs so that reification ends."[11]

The doe speaks, the deer listens: "You, deer!
Abandon this forest and be a wanderer."

The speaking of the doe is the manifestation of emptiness in impermanence and ungraspability; the listening of the deer represents inwardly silencing conceptual description reifying things. When the intelligence comes to understand that nothing can be grasped or possessed, it is induced to let go of its holdings and thus free itself from thralldom to the realm of the senses. The *Sandhinirmocana-sutra* says, "Those who pursue thoughts cannot think of, or assess, or believe in the character of the ultimate truth that is beyond the sphere of all thought and deliberation."[12]

As it sprints away,
the hooves of the deer cannot be seen;
Bhusuku says so, but it enters not the ignorant mind.

Sprinting away represents transcending the world. Leaving no tracks means that transcendence is not an act of rejection, not a program of ascetic denial, but a departure from subjective views and illusions. Attachment to detachment is not freedom; even less so is attachment to masochistic self-indulgence in the name of mortification.

Yet even though this is authoritatively stated, the point is not understood by the ignorant, who prefer to follow tracks. When the emperor of China, a lavish patron of Buddhist churches, asked the founder of Zen what the highest meaning of the holy truths is, the Zen founder replied, "Empty, nothing holy." When the emperor failed to understand, the Zen founder left the country; but as a later commentator said, "How could he avoid the growth of a thicket of brambles?" This is Bhusuku's point. As a contemporary Indian saying has it, "Buddha told people not to worship anything, and then they began to worship him."

7

KAHNU

The road was blocked by the vowels and consonants;
Seeing that, Kahnu was saddened.
Where can Kahnu go to make an abode?
He is unattached to any object of mind.
The three of them, they three are separate;
Kahnu says, "The world is broken!"
Whatever has come has gone;
In the forest of lingering attachment,
Kahnu was sad.
Kahnu is here, nearby, in the city of the Victor;
Kahnu says, "Infatuation doesn't enter my mind."

The road was blocked by the vowels and consonants;
Seeing that, Kahnu was saddened.

The vowels and consonants represent conventionalized cognition and understanding, structured by language and conceptualization. These "block the road" in the sense that when they capture all of our attention, they obstruct formless intuitive perception and understanding.

To be "saddened" by this recognition is to realize the limitations of conditioned mental constructions. As in the case of other exercises in observation of limitation, the purpose here is to arouse the *bodhicitta* or thought of enlightenment.

Where can Kahnu go to make an abode?
He is unattached to any object of mind.

Intelligent contemplation of impermanence is a basic Buddhist practice exercised for the purpose of cultivating nonattachment, as a means of freeing the mind from the compulsive force of habitual involvement in objects of thought and feeling. The *Diamond-sutra* says, "One should activate the mind without dwelling on anything."

The three of them, they three are separate;
Kahnu says, "The world is broken!"

This couplet represents another method of meditation. Here the "three" are the organs, objects, and consciousnesses of the senses. The practitioner develops a keen inner sense of emptiness through meditating on the relativity of sense organs, sense objects, and sense consciousnesses.

To arrive at the inconceivable state of nonconceptual cognition, one contemplates organs of sense without consciousness or object, consciousness of sense without organs or objects, and objects of sense without organs or consciousnesses. Because all experience consists of combinations of these three, no one of them can be grasped in itself. Since no one can be grasped in itself, what is there to combine?

Naturally, it must be kept in mind that this is an exercise in attention, not philosophical rhetoric. The use of logic is not to arrive at conceptual resolutions, but to maneuver the attention in such a way as to focus inconceivable insights beyond the domain of discursive thought.

Whatever has come has gone;
In the forest of lingering attachment,
Kahnu was sad.

Having entered the domain of extraordinary perceptions and intimations of spiritual experience, it is again necessary to meditate seriously on transience, so as to be free of clinging attachment to relative phenomena, however abstract or ethereal they may be. A Zen proverb says, "It is comparatively easy to rise higher with every step; it is harder to let go of each state of mind." Kahnu's "sadness" mimes the condition of one who had become infatuated with a temporary spiritual state, and therefore experiences its passing as a loss.

Kahnu is here, nearby, in the city of the Victor;
Kahnu says, "Infatuation doesn't enter my mind."

The final couplet illustrates the condition of one who has gone beyond infatuation with all phenomena, both mundane and transmundane.

The Victor is an epithet of a Buddha, one who has overcome delusion. The domain of enlightenment is "nearby" in our innermost mind and our objective environment everywhere. The Chinese Zen master Kuei-shan said, "As long as feelings do not stick to things, how can things hinder you?"

8

KAMBALAMBARA

The boat of compassion is filled with gold;
There is no place to keep any silver.
Sail, Kamali, up to the sky!
When life is gone, how can it return?
When the peg is uprooted and the rope unraveled,
Sail off, O Kamali, having asked a true guide.
Riding on the prow of the boat,
he seeks in the four directions;
Without an oar, how can he row?

The boat of compassion is filled with gold;
There is no place to keep any silver.

Silver represents the relative thought of enlightenment, which is intellectual understanding of the human predicament and the consequent aspiration to rise above it. Gold represents the absolute thought of enlightenment, which is intuitive gnosis of ultimate truth.

Buddhism distinguishes three kinds of compassion. There is sentimental compassion, which is personal and emotional, taking the troubles of oneself and others at face value. Then there is dreamlike compassion, which is austere and visionary, regarding human problems as results of illusion. Finally there is objectless compassion, which is natural, spontaneous, and unbiased by emotionalized conceptions of persons as objects of compassion.

This couplet sings of objectless compassion, which can only come about through experiential realization of the absolute truth, transcending psychologically conditioned notions and sentiments. This is why the adept says that the boat of compassion is filled with gold and has no more room for silver. Here he echoes the teaching of Nagarjuna, the seminal Buddhist writer on emptiness, who stated that true emptiness *is* true compassion.

Sail, Kamali, up to the sky!
When life is gone, how can it return?

Kamali is a vernacular or familiar form of the poet's name. He urges himself to "sail up to the sky," in the sense of rising above views of the world, to realize emptiness.

Here it is important to distinguish between the usage of the word "sky" as representing emptiness *(sunyata),* which Buddhists consider ultimate truth, and its usage in terms such as "absorption in the plane of the sky" *(gagana-tala-samadhz),* which represent exercises in abstraction.

The key to determining which meaning is intended is in the second line of the couplet. Prince Siddhartha did not attain liberation and enlightenment and become Buddha until he gave up pursuing yogic trances as aims in themselves, realizing that they are still impermanent.

Here the Tantric adept also points out that this life is our only chance for enlightenment, a manner of teaching also common to Zen masters of the Far East. Later Lamaism notwithstanding, there is even a Tibetan proverb that says, "No one has the power to be born again and again."

The self-exhortation method of meditation represented here is another feature of this teaching that is also practiced in Zen. A model example in the classic *koan* collection *No Barrier* relates that every day Zen master Ruiyan would call to himself and answer himself; then he would say to himself, "Be awake, be alert!" "Yes!" "From now on, don't be fooled by anyone!" "Yes! Yes!"

When the peg is uprooted and the rope unraveled,
Sail off, O Kamali, having asked a true guide.

The peg is a false sense of permanence and stability. The unraveling of the rope represents analytic meditation such as that explained in the preceding song by Kahnu.

A man walking at night sees a piece of rope in the road. In the dark, he thinks it is a snake, and is frightened. This stands for the conceptualized nature of things; we conceive things to be such and so, describe them thus in our minds, and react to our own descriptions.

On closer examination, it is not a snake; it is only a piece of rope. This stands for the relative nature of things. This is the realm of conditional existence as is, apart from what we may imagine subjectively.

On yet closer analysis, the "rope" is actually a name for a bundle of fibers twisted together, perceived and used as a single entity. This stands for the absolute nature of things, the sense in which nothing exists of itself, but only as a temporary association of interdependent elements.

This rope metaphor is a classical contemplation method of Buddhist Yoga, designed to dissolve the opacity of concrete pseudo-absoluteness projected on objects by the unreflective mind still in the stage of naive realism. It is referred to elsewhere in these Tantric songs, and is also widely represented in Far Eastern Buddhism, especially T'ien-t'ai "stopping and seeing" practices, and certain types of Zen *koan* meditation.

Riding on the prow of the boat,
he seeks in the four directions;
Without an oar, how can he row?

Seeking in the four directions refers to meditation on the sense in which things conditionally exist, the sense in which things do not absolutely exist, the sense in which things neither exist nor do not exist, and the sense in which things both exist and do not exist.

This exercise is also basic to T'ien-t'ai Buddhism, and is found in Zen *koans.* Although the setup used may often take the form of logical propositions, the purpose of the practice is not philosophical or rhetorical, but psychological. It is a guide to meditation method, which the Tantric adept here likens to an oar propelling a boat onward, as the technique propels inner perception in its progress toward refinement.

The boat is pressed on either side, left and right;
On the way the Great Ecstasy has been found.

Pursuing the "four direction" meditation, "either side, left and right," can be understood to refer to existence and non-existence. Combining this with the "energy channel" meditation spoken of earlier and evidently alluded to here, the left and right channels, of dalliance and perception, can be used as receptacles of the experiences witnessed in the process of the "four direction" meditations, each step of which provokes specific different experiences.

The inner visionary representations of these experiences, as they are registered in the channels of perception and dalliance, are then pressed into the central channel, that is the channel of purification, where they are resolved, clarified, and purified.

The Great Ecstasy that is found in the purification channel is the subtle bliss of disentanglement and liberation characteristic of the realization of emptiness.

The "way" here has two levels of meaning, both indicated by the esoteric terminology. Emptiness is the "Middle Way" between attachment and rejection, affirmation and denial. The middle channel of purification thus symbolically stands for the realization of emptiness, by which the mind is purified of biased views.

Concretely, in Tantric practice, it technically stands for the inner visualization in which the contemplation of emptiness is carried out and formless insight is subtly registered in the mindbody continuum.

This is beautifully illustrated in a Zen *koan* in the famous collection known as *The Blue Cliff Record.* One day a Zen master "went wandering in the mountains." When he returned, a disciple asked him where he had been. "Wandering in the mountains," he said. "Where did you go?" the disciple asked.

"First I went pursuing the fragrant grasses," replied the master; "then I returned following the falling flowers." The disciple said, "How springlike!" But the master said, "Cooler than autumn dew dripping on the lotus."

In terms of inner visualization meditation, wandering in the mountains means psychic experience within the energy network visualized in the place of one's own physical body. The fragrant grasses and the falling flowers refer to the channels of perception and dalliance. The disciple's reaction is still in the vein of dalliance ("warm"), so the master corrects him in the vein of purification ("cool").

9

KAHNU

The pillar, so firm, is broken;
The various fastenings encircling it are torn away.
Kahnu makes love, drunk with wine;
In the lotus forest of spontaneity,
he is extremely happy.
As when an elephant bull makes love to a cow,
So does suchness rain like the elephant's sweat.
The six courses are all inherently pure,
Unstained in the least by being and nonbeing.
The treasure of the ten powers
is collected in the ten directions:
Tame the elephant of ignorance, by being unaffected.

The pillar, so firm, is broken;
The various fastenings encircling it are torn away.

This couplet illustrates a meditative exercise in transcending subjectivity, applied to both body and mind. In meditating on the body, one mentally reduces one's physical existence to elements, seeing thereby through the death of the self. In meditating on the mind, the temporally acquired mentality is "deconstructed" by analyzing the cultural, social, and personal factors that have conditioned and formed it.

Kahnu makes love, drunk with wine;
In the lotus forest of spontaneity,
he is extremely happy.

Making love symbolizes union with emptiness. Inebriation symbolizes having nothing hanging on one's mind, having one's mind off things. Wine stands for the subtle euphoria of nirvana.

The lotus forest of spontaneity is the experience of life after nirvana. Extreme happiness refers to the condition of one who has escaped the prison of artificialities.

As when an elephant bull makes love to a cow,
So does suchness rain like the elephant's sweat.

Suchness, *tathata* in both Sanskrit and Bengali, means actuality as directly witnessed without conceptualization. Because it is not limited by the filtration of conceptual processing, the experience called "suchness" gives the impression of extraordinary richness and abundance.

The six courses are all inherently pure,
Unstained in the least by being and nonbeing.

The six courses are states of mind represented by animals, ghosts, denizens of hell, human beings, celestial beings, and antigods. Animals symbolize ignorance and folly, ghosts symbolize cupidity and greediness, antigods symbolize aggression and hatred, human beings symbolize socialization, and celestial beings symbolize meditative states. These six are often conventionally used to stand for the whole range of conditioned states, and in various combinations may be employed to describe psychological complexes.

Ordinarily the path of Buddhism is first represented as transcendence of these six courses of conditioning. In the Buddhist practice known as stopping or cessation, the mind ceases its active occupation with conditioned states. In the complementary practice known as seeing or contemplation, the compulsiveness of six courses is undermined by viewing them as inherently empty of absolute existence by the very fact of their dependence on conditions.

In accord with the two meditative modes of stopping and seeing, or cessation and contemplation, the meaning of "pure" is twofold. In the state of stopping or cessation of thought, everything seems clear, because there is no judgment and comparison. In the process of seeing and contemplating the ultimate nature of things, insight penetrates the vanity of subjective imagination, while intellect comprehends the inevitable end of all that is caused.

Because conditioned phenomena depend on other things, they have no absolute intrinsic existence of their own; thus they are "unstained by being." Insofar as they do exist relatively when causal conditions coalesce, phenomena are not absolutely nonexistent either, so they are "unstained by nonbeing." This is one way Buddhism defines the Middle Way, which is none other than true emptiness.

The treasure of the ten powers
is collected in the ten directions:
Tame the elephant of ignorance, by being unaffected.

The ten powers are powers of knowledge characteristic of complete Buddhas. Together, they are referred to as the consummate all-knowledge or omniscience of Buddhas, which they use to enlighten others. The first one is knowledge of what is true and what is not. Second is knowledge of the results of actions. Third is knowlege of various interests. Fourth is knowledge of various realms. Fifth is knowledge of different faculties, higher and lower.

The sixth power is knowledge of all destinations, or consequences of various different ways of life. Seventh is knowledge of all states of meditation and concentration, including how they get polluted, how they are purified, and how to enter into them and emerge from them. Eighth is knowledge of past history. Ninth is knowledge of others' conditions. Tenth is knowledge of ending contamination, which means being free from psychological affliction in the midst of all experience, mundane or supramundane.

The ten directions represent the totality of the relative universe, including both mental and material aspects. The treasure of the ten powers of knowledge is "collected" in the ten directions in the sense that the relative universe is the "mine" from which these knowledges are extracted.

By the same token, the relative universe "conceals" these knowledges from the eye that only looks at superficial appearances and fails to descry underlying patterns. For this reason it is said that the fundamental substance of illusion and enlightenment is one and the same; the difference between folly and wisdom lies in how the individual handles it.

This is a basic perspective of Mahayana Buddhism, and a primary meaning of Tantra, which is translated into Chinese as "fundamental continuity." The relative thought of enlightenment is cultivated on the basis of this understanding, and the absolute thought of enlightenment is awakened through perception of this continuity.

A key to overcoming the basic ignorance of self-contained subjectivity, and thus perceiving the "fundamental continuity" and there beginning the process of disinterring the ten knowledges from throughout the universe, is suggested in the final line of the adept's song—"by being unaffected." When the blinding force of automatic judgment and emotional reaction is undermined by intelligent nonparticipation, then attention can be stabilized and greater objectivity can be realized. This process is also called "stopping and seeing."

10

KAHNU

Outside the city is your hut, Gypsy woman;
You go on touching the Brahmin scholar.
Hey, Gypsy woman! I'll be with you; live with me!
Kahnu the hated is a naked mendicant.
A single lotus with sixty-four petals;
Climbing onto it, the destitute Gypsy woman dances.
O Gypsy woman, I ask you about true being;
In whose boat, O Gypsy, do you come and go?
The Gypsy woman sells her mandolin,
and has no wicker basket;
She's discarded her dancer's paraphernalia
right in front of you.
O Gypsy woman, I'm a naked mendicant!
From you I have gotten a garland of bones.
Breaking the tank,
the Gypsy woman eats the lotus root;
I kill the Gypsy woman, I take life.

Outside the city is your hut, Gypsy woman;
You go on touching the Brahmin scholar.

The Gypsy woman symbolically stands for the ultimate self-lessness (inherent identitylessness) and emptiness (inherent nonabsoluteness) of temporal phenomena. This subtle spiritual perception is "outside the city," beyond the limits and bounds of the edifice of conventional reality as construed by the historically and culturally conditioned thought habit and worldview. This is why the *Sandhinirmocana-sutra* says that, "The ultimate truth transcends all objects of thought and deliberation."

The Gypsy woman is an "outcaste," rejected by the orthodox Brahmin scholar of conventional thinking. "Someone in ignorance who clings to rhetoric," continues the *Sandhinirmocanasutra,* "because of an overwhelming interest in words, thus cannot think of, or assess, or believe in the pleasure of holy silence with inner tranquility."[13] And yet the "scholar's" edifice of thought, being itself relative and conditioned, has no absolute existence of its own; in Buddhist terms, it is ultimately "empty." So the "Gypsy woman" of emptiness "keeps on touching" the "Brahmin scholar" of form.

Hey, Gypsy woman! I'll be with you; live with me!
Kahnu the hated is a naked mendicant.

To realize communion with objective emptiness, the Buddhist first becomes inwardly empty; thus "I'll be with you; live with me!" This is not, however, to escape reality, but rather to face reality more directly; more directly, that is, than is possible through a rigidly self-limiting framework of fixed assumptions and descriptions. This is a matter of recovering original freedom of perspective and potential from herd-instinct conformism to coercive training and unexamined habit.

Such is the nature of convention, nevertheless, that conformism is part of its operation. Thus a certain price is to be paid for departure from the circle of familiarity and acceptance. Here that price is summed up in the word "hated." This is not necessarily intended literally, although it is not unknown for hatred to be visited upon the unconventional. In a more subtle sense, "hated" means that one's integrity is not dependent upon the views of others.

The naked mendicant is the mind that is not clothed by worldly thought habit and not employed by worldly compulsion. The famous Sung dynasty Chinese Zen master Yuan-wu, writing about the same time as these Bengali Siddhas, often used the expression "bare and untrammeled, naked and free" to describe the state of the mind not veiled by presumption or preconception and not clouded by inner or outer conversation.

A single lotus with sixty-four petals;
Climbing onto it, the destitute Gypsy woman dances.

Sixty-four is the total number of wordly arts and sciences; the total number of erotic arts is also said to be sixty-four. One lotus with sixty-four petals represents the mind-body continuum and its manifold, complex capacities.

Destitution symbolizes nonattachment, which means freedom from obsessiveness. This characterizes the realization of selflessness and emptiness, which stand for the fluidity of the liberated mind.

The "Gypsy" dancing illustrates the dynamic nature of selflessness and emptiness. These terms, in their practical dimensions, do not denote negative states of suppression or withdrawal, but rather the renewable, constructive ability to operate without unconsciously losing perception and creativity to the lull of repetitious habit.

Imagery of enlightening beings with many faces, hands, and implements frequently appears in Tantric and other Buddhist art, reflecting the versatility and richness of human development believed to be possible in the aftermath of psychological, intellectual, and spiritual liberation.

O Gypsy woman, I ask you about true being;
In whose boat, O Gypsy, do you come and go?

According to the *prajnaparamita* teaching, matter is emptiness, and emptiness is matter; the same is true, furthermore, of sensation, perception, conception, and consciousness. Thus being and emptiness are identified, metaphysically and intuitively, as a basis for practical exercises, contemplation, and insight.

On one level, being is the "vehicle" in which "emptiness" is conveyed, to the contemplative eye seeing into metaphysical reality. On another level, the "unidentified" mind that does not cling to anything possessively has a pragmatic kind of "emptiness" in it, even while in the midst of material forms, sensations, perceptions, conceptions, and consciousness. As in the Taoist image of the "empty boat," this inner emptiness, in Buddhist terms, is what the classical Zen master Lin-chi called "not taking on the delusions of others."

In terms of Buddhist Yoga, all these phenomena have relative existence, but their existence as we picture and define them to ourselves is subjective and conditional. So this existence is nonexistent in absolutely objective reality. By detachment from its conceptual description of things, the mind is enabled to perceive and conceive in ways not defined in that description; and it is also enabled to sense absolute emptiness intuitively.

The question "in whose boat do you come and go" implies that emptiness should not be sought in abstract nothingness outside or other than existence, or in quietism separated from the world. This theme is common to universalist Buddhism, both in the scriptures and the works of the schools.

The question "whose boat" also suggests that in order to liberate the mind from arbitrary restrictions due to historical conditioning, it is imperative to know what that conditioning is. This Buddhist self-analysis includes individual and collective or interactive dimensions of personal and social evolution and development, as shown in illustrative stories about conditions in past lives and other worlds frequently found in classical and vernacular Buddhist literature.

The Gypsy woman sells her mandolin,
and has no wicker basket;
She's discarded her dancer's paraphernalia
right in front of you.

Abandoning instruments, implements, and paraphernalia symbolizes abandoning the means when the end has been reached. This happens "right in front of you" in the sense that now your perception of truth is not limited by the medium of symbol and method, but is experienced as direct witness.

O Gypsy woman, I'm a naked mendicant!
From you I have gotten a garland of bones.

Having divested oneself of psychological and intellectual holdings, one's perceptions and intuitions are not obscured by an overlay of arbitrary thought-habit, and one's energy and attention are not in the employ of worldly ambitions. From the experiential realization of emptiness, the superficial "flesh" of subjective illusions is stripped away, leaving the bare "bones" of objective truth.

Breaking the tank,
the Gypsy woman eats the lotus root;
I kill the Gypsy woman, I take life.

According to Nagarjuna, the master expositor of emptiness, the Buddhas have declared that departure from all views is emptiness, but those who take emptiness for a view cannot be cured. Thus the doctrine of emptiness says that things are not as we think them to be, and yet they are not nothing.

When the contemplation of emptiness slips unconsciously into nothingness, the regenerative potential of the emptiness experience is nullified. This pseudo-emptiness, while subjectively comfortable, is ultimately destructive to social, psychological, and spiritual integrity. In that sense, of "emptiness" taken to an extreme, the "Gypsy" breaks the vessel of life and consumes the root of life. So the adept "kills the Gypsy woman" and thus "takes life." In Zen terms, first one "breaks up the home and scatters the family," then one "comes to understand how to make a living."

11

KRISHNA

The energy in the channels is strong,
suspended in space;
The unbeaten drum is played
in the call of the valiant one.
Krishna the naked yogi has entered into practice;
In uniformity he moves freely
through the city of the body.
The vowels and consonants
are bell-anklets on the feet;
The sun and moon are ornamental bangles.
Abandon lust, hatred, and folly;
Take supreme liberation, a garland of pearls.
Killing mother-in-law, sister,
and sister-in-law at home,
Killing mother,
Krishna has become a naked mendicant.

The energy in the channels is strong,
suspended in space;
The unbeaten drum is played
in the call of the valiant one.

The channels here are the energy channels visualized in the body, as explained earlier. When the energy in the channels is strong, that means the visualization is fully developed. "Suspended in space" means that the visualization of the energy channels is based on emptiness, and also that it supersedes ordinary awareness of the physical body and surroundings.

The call of the valiant one is what is commonly referred to as the "lion's roar," meaning the Buddhist teaching of emptiness, which overcomes all illusions, as a valiant warrior overcomes enemies. The drum is also a common symbol of Buddhist teaching; in this case it is said to be played "unbeaten" in the sense that emptiness, being intrinsic to relativity and not anything in itself, is therefore not relative to anything.

Krishna the naked yogi has entered into practice;
In uniformity he moves freely
through the city of the body.

The yogi's nakedness represents freedom from attachment, having no psychological holdings. If one enters into Tantric practice greedy for secrets and powers, that will prevent enlightenment. Thus it is necessary for the yogi to be "naked" as a prerequisite to success in this practice.

Mental "travel" through the body is part of Tantric visualization practice, utilizing the network of energy channels centered on the three main channels. When the attention alights on different points, this stimulates different psychic experiences; "uniformity" here refers to psychological equanimity, which enables the yogi to "move freely" through the energy body without getting hung up on any particular experience.

The vowels and consonants
are bell-anklets on the feet;
The sun and moon are ornamental bangles.

The vowels and consonants represent energy and matter, the universe of form and structure. The sun and moon are absolute and relative thought of enlightenment, formless awakening of mind based on intuition of absolute truth and formal awakening of mind based on analysis of relative truth. Both the life of the ordinary world (vowels and consonants) as well as the life of spiritual development (sun and moon) are experienced as adornments from the point of view of the ethereal essence of consciousness centered in emptiness.

Abandon lust, hatred, and folly;
Take supreme liberation, a garland of pearls.

Lust, hatred, and folly are traditionally described as the "three poisons" at the root of unnecessary human suffering. Liberation from these three poisons is a basic aim of Buddhism; this is repeated even after the exalted vision of the preceding couplet because lust, hatred, and folly can also be generated from ignorant attitudes toward "spiritual" experience, just as they can derive from an ignorant relation to life experience in the material world.

Killing mother-in-law, sister,
and sister-in-law at home,
Killing mother,
Krishna has become a naked mendicant.

Killing is a standard symbol for realization of impermanence, for detachment, and for transcendence. This couplet follows up on the preceding. The ninth-century Chinese Zen master Linchi said, "If you want to attain objective vision and understanding, just do not take on the confusion of others. Whatever you meet, inwardly and outwardly, immediately kill. If you meet Buddha, kill Buddha; if you meet a Zen master, kill the Zen master; if you meet a saint, kill the saint. If you meet your parents, kill your parents; if you meet your relatives, kill your relatives. Only then can you attain liberation, and penetrate through to freedom, without being constrained by things." The use of language which, however symbolic, is nevertheless harsh and even shocking, is a technique common to Tantric and Zen Buddhism, used to jar the consciousness out of the self-hypnotic mental lethargy known in Buddhist Yoga as "the lull of words."

12

KRISHNA

I play a game of chess on the board of compassion;
The true teacher, by enlightenment,
has overcome the power of the world.
The deuce is removed, the king is slain;
By the instruction of the teacher,
Krishna is near the winner's circle.
Breaking through the front line, I slay the pawns; Mounting an elephant, I stir up five people.
The king is extinguished by wisdom;
With certainty, the power of the world is overcome.
Krishna says, "I give a good gambling stake:
Surveying the sixty-four squares on the chessboard,
I take it."

I play a game of chess on the board of compassion;
The true teacher, by enlightenment,
has overcome the power of the world.

The board of compassion is the world as it is experienced by the liberated Buddhist who can no longer be confused by things of the world. The exercise of free compassion is metaphorically represented as "play" because it is a spontaneous expression of transcendental independence. The Japanese Zen master Hakuin wrote, "Enlightening beings of the higher vehicle do not dwell in the state of result they have realized; from the ocean of effortlessness, they radiate unconditional great compassion. . . . This is what is called coming back within going away, going away within coming back."[14]

The deuce is removed, the king is slain;
By the instruction of the teacher,
Krishna is near the winner's circle.

The "deuce" stands for dualistic thinking; removing the deuce means overcoming illusory dualism. The "king" is egocentrism; slaying the king means overcoming self-centered habits of thinking, behaving, and processing experience. The winner's circle is the realm of enlightenment.

Nonduality and objectivity are characteristics of compassion in the Buddhist sense of the word, as illustrated by Zen master Hakuin: "Powerful enlightening beings spin the wheel of the principle of nonduality of light and dark. In the midst of the red dust, ashes on the head and mud on the face, they act freely in the company of sound and form; like a lotus blossom whose color and fragrance become fresher and clearer in fire, they go into the marketplace extending their hands, acting for others.

"This is what is called being on the road without leaving home, leaving home without being on the road."[14]

Breaking through the front line, I slay the pawns; Mounting an elephant, I stir up five people.

The front line is the surface of things, or things as they seem to be. The pawns are the constituent elements of things. Breaking through the front line and slaying the pawns means seeing through the outward aspects of things by penetrating analysis of the elements of events.

According to Munidatta, the elephant stands for mindfulness of things as they really are, and the five people stand for the five clusters (form, feeling, perception, habit, and consciousness), and the objects of the five elementary senses. Knowing things as they really are uproots the notion of selfhood in the five clusters and the overmastering influence of the objects of the five senses.

The king is extinguished by wisdom;
With certainty, the power of the world is overcome.

The word for wisdom used here, *mati,* also means intelligence and understanding, both in Sanskrit and Old Bengali. The "king," can also be translated "the idol," highlighting its symbolic meaning. One point of saying that the "king" or dominant egotism is extinguished by wisdom or intelligence is to counter the notion that selflessness refers to a zombielike state achieved by simple mortification, or a condition of compulsive servility engineered by operant conditioning.

In practical terms, the egotistic orientation is not undermined by bullying, abasement, or suppression of individuality. These procedures, which are often found in authoritarian cults, actually tend to harden the shell of the ego, as it perversely aggrandizes itself through abasement, supposing this to be holiness.

In the same way, the "power of the world," the allure, fascination, or distraction of material senses, is not to be definitively overcome by procedures whose essential technique is denial or isolation from the world. In terms of practical philosophy, this means that "emptiness" is not nothingness; it is not realized by bludgeoning oneself senseless, or by puzzling oneself witless, but by certitude of insight into absolute truth.

"With certainty" means "certainly," describing the annihilation of king ego-centrism by means of wisdom. In Zen as well as Tantric symbolism, this intelligence, this wisdom, is symbolized by an inconceivably sharp sword.

**Krishna says, "I give a good gambling stake:
Surveying the sixty-four squares on the chessboard,
I take it."**

The "good gambling stake" given by the one who has already overcome the world and attained freedom is the rededication of purified, liberated, and enlightened thought, word, and deed to the liberation of others.

According to Buddhist teaching, there are people whom even Buddhas cannot help. Dedication to the liberation of others cannot, therefore, be practically undertaken in the spirit of expectation. This pertinent fact of life is encapsulated in the playful reference to the bodhisattva enterprise as a "gamble."

The sixty-four squares of the board symbolically represent the sum total of the arts and sciences, or the whole potential accessible to humankind. The adept returning to the world after liberation "surveys" the sixty-four squares to observe the total context of human activities and possibilities, and see what move might be made where, with what effects.

Based on this knowledge, both general and particular, the adept then "takes" the "move," even "takes" the whole board, acting appropriately to each setting, regarding all sixty-four squares as having value, actual or potential.

13

KRISHNA

The Three Refuges are made a boat
by the One with Eight Children;
His own body compassion, emptiness is his wife.
Having crossed over the ocean of existence,
it is like an illusion, a dream;
The central current is deeply considered
during the crossing over.
With the Five Tathagatas as oars,
Krishna's body crosses the net of illusion.
Scent, texture, taste, however they may be,
Are like dreams without sleep.
Mind the sailor, emptiness the boat,
Krishna has gone off, with great bliss.

The Three Refuges are made a boat
by the One with Eight Children;
His own body compassion, emptiness is his wife.

In Sanskrit the Three Refuges are called Buddha, Dharma, and Sangha. On one level, these terms refer to an enlightened exemplar (Buddha), an enlightening teaching (Dharma), and a harmonious communion of people (Sangha) attuned to the teaching. On the level of personal realization, the Buddha is the awakened mind, the Dharma is objective reality, and the Sangha consists of all living beings.

The One with Eight Children is what is called *amalavijnana* in Sanskrit, meaning "Pure Consciousness." According to Buddhist psychology this subtends eight consciousnesses: five basic sense consciousnesses, cognitive consciousness, intellect, and a repository or storage consciousness. As differentiations of function, these eight consciousnesses may be pictured as deriving from the ninth, or pure consciousness; so this pure consciousness is referred to as "the one with eight children."

The *Sandhinirmocana-sutra* says of this pure consciousness, "It is the basis of the adornments of the enlightened. Its pathways are mindfulness and knowledge, its vehicles are great tranquility and subtle observation. Its entrances are the great liberations of emptiness, signlessness, and wishlessness, and its adornments are infinite virtues."[15]

The boat is a symbol of a vehicle or means of deliverance, of liberation. It is pure consciousness that brings the Three Refuges to life and makes them into a way to freedom. Without this living element, "Buddha" is an icon, "Dharma" is a doctrine, and "Sangha" is a business or social club. The *Sandhinirmocanasutra* explains, "With supremely pure awareness, the awakened one is attached neither to the mundane nor to the supramundane. He proceeds according to formless truth, and dwells in the abode of the enlightened."[16]

The consummation of enlightenment is conventionally described as a wedding of insight and compassion, or wisdom and skill in expedient means. In these terms, insight and wisdom refer to the fluid or ethereal aspect of emptiness, while compassion and skill in means refer to the concrete or localized manifestation of emptiness, which is the relativity of existence. Realization of emptiness, in the Buddhist sense, therefore implies liberation from absolutist fixations, which enables the mind thus awakened to operate more freely.

Hence the wedding of compassion and emptiness means the capacity to be present and active in the world without becoming imprisoned in the process. This is the description of the Buddhist ideal of the bodhisattva or enlightening being, who is in the world but not of the world.

Having crossed over the ocean of existence,
it is like an illusion, a dream;
The central current is deeply considered
during the crossing over.

The word "illusion" is used here, as often in Buddhist literature, in the manner of magicians, for whom the word means a deception of the senses. The effect depends upon the brain's habit of selecting, organizing, and interpreting data into familiar representations; the magician or illusionist deceives the audience by manipulating attention, directing and diverting it in order to produce calculated effects in the minds of observers.

A dream is also usually considered a subjective perception of something that is not objectively there, an organization of neurological activity or data into a representation of experience. Whether a dream is thought of as a random release of energy, as a reflection of everyday life, or as a mirror of unconscious urges, what Buddhist literature generally refers to by the image of a dream is the phenomenon of experiencing what seems to be actually real and yet is not.

The metaphors of the illusion and the dream, as used in Buddhist teaching, thus refer to the mentally constructed nature of the world as we conceive of it. We do not perceive objective reality directly and wholly; our brains select, edit, and organize the data of our senses into conceivable, manageable representations. It is in this sense, in reference to how we construe things, that Buddhist scripture says that the world is only mind, or only consciousness, or only representation.

The particular ways in which individual and collective minds construe information are historically conditioned by culture, society, and personal experience. Born into a particular culture in a particular time, one learns to perceive the world, and to think about it, in a manner conforming to that culture in that time. In a condition of "total immersion" from infancy and therefore having no basis of comparison, one subconsciously absolutizes the world one learns to perceive.

Even as one matures within a particular culture, there is no obvious way of knowing that this "world" is an interpretation, a mental construction. The internalized worldview filters experience in such a way as to exclude disruptive incongruity, preserve its own structure intact, and maintain the continuity of the habit of thought into which it has been conditioned. It is only after "having crossed over," or having gotten past the boundaries of self-reflection, having ceased to absolutize a worldview, that one can see its subjective nature, its illusionlike or dream-like quality.

This realization might be described as a kind of liberation, but it is not yet enlightenment. In penetrating the illusion of objectivity in subjective absolutism, there is a peril of swinging from a relative extreme of attachment to an opposite extreme of rejection. Then the result is not freedom from delusion, but simply disillusion; instead of releasing creative vision and potential, it breeds destructive cynicism and nihilism.

That problem of extremism, often mentioned in Buddhist technical literature, is why "the central current is deeply considered during the crossing over." No longer able to cling to the world as absolute, nevertheless one does not deny the world as relative. Neither does one deny the actuality of all sorts of views of the world, and their effects on people's minds and behavior, however unrealistic any particular views may be. Integrating these perspectives without bias is the Middle Way, the "central current." In Mahayana Buddhism, this is often referred to in general pragmatic terms as "neither grasping nor rejecting."

With the Five Tathagatas as oars,
Krishna's body crosses the net of illusion.

Tathagata is another word for a Buddha, referring to attainment and expression of objective reality. The Five Tathagatas are the so-called Dhyani Buddhas or Meditation Buddhas: Vairocana, Ratnasambhava, Amoghasiddhi, Akshobhya, and Amitayur. These names are associated with specific aspects of enlightened knowledge and are invoked in Tantric meditation methodology.

Vairocana, "The Illuminator" or "Cosmic Sun," associated with cognition of the essential nature of the cosmos, is visualized in the forehead. Ratnasambhava, "Made of Jewels," associated with cognition of equality, is visualized in the right shoulder. Amoghasiddhi, "Impeccable Accomplishment," associated with practical knowledge, is visualized in the left shoulder. Akshobhya, "The Immovable One," associated with mirrorlike cognition, is visualized in the heart. Amitayur, "Infinite Life," associated with precise observational cognition, is visualized in the throat.

This visualization practice involves a different way of experiencing the body, or the sense of physical being, through positive transformation of its mental basis. Certain symbolic gestures, sounds, prayers, thoughts, images, and color associations may also be used to help the actualization of transformation. In this way, as the personal experience of being is refined, the mind-body complex is propelled beyond the confines imposed by the illusion of absoluteness.

Scent, texture, taste, however they may be,
Are like dreams without sleep.

The similarity of ordinary sense experience to that of dreams lies in the general process of representation, and in the habit of taking representation for reality. Just as we ordinarily don't know we are dreaming when we are dreaming, Buddhists say, we ordinarily don't realize we are reacting to subjective views when we think we are experiencing objective reality.

When we are awake (in the ordinary sense of the word), our brains normally have greater control over the images they hold than they do when we are asleep. While our waking brains may be able to control images, in the sense of keeping them steady, they do not necessarily have control over this control. That is to say, the way in which our brains organize and maintain our pictures of the world is a product of both biological and social inheritance and conditioning.

In this sense, as we are we ultimately have no more "control" over our experience of ourselves and our world, and no more contact with objective reality, in the state in which we think we are "awake" than we do when we are asleep and dreaming. This is why Buddhists try to become more conscious, more awake; not just because dreams are not real, but because the full potential of human intelligence and creativity only becomes accessible when consciousness emerges from the shell of fixation on imagined realities and preoccupation with preconceptions.

Deliberate transformation of consciousness, performed by Tantric Buddhists in both waking and dreaming meditation, is an exercise in will and attention, undertaken in order to overcome the power over the mind exerted by the automatic repetition of inherited and conditioned worldviews.

Mind the sailor, emptiness the boat,
Krishna has gone off, with great bliss.

Through insight into emptiness and conscious restructuring of experience, the mind is emancipated from slavery to instinct and conditioning, and develops the capacity of autonomy and free will. In Zen Buddhism, this capacity is called the director, or the host; in Tantric Buddhism, this may be referred to as the *vajradhara,* the thunderbolt-bearer, holder of power.

Were it not for fluidity, which is the quality of emptiness, the mind would have no means of conscious transformation and creative development. Were there no direction, which is the nature of will, fluidity would degenerate into vulnerability, irresoluteness, and lack of meaning and purpose.

Thus it is with "mind the sailor" and "emptiness the boat" that the adept has "gone off" beyond the range of worldly illusions, with the "great bliss" of having first escaped from a suffocating prison, and then found an inexhaustible source of treasures.

14

DOMBI

Between the Ganges and the Yamuna,
there runs a river:
Submerged in it, the outcaste yogini
effortlessly reaches the other shore.
Sail on, Gypsy, sail on;
there's been a delay on the way.
At the lotus feet of the true teacher,
you will go again to the city of the Victorious.
The five oars are put down,
a rope is tied to the back of the boat;
With the sky for a pot, I bail water,
so it doesn't get in through the cracks.
The moon and sun are the mast
upon which creation is unfurled and wrapped up;
The two courses, left and right, do not appear good;
let one sail on at will.
Without a penny, without a dime,
one reaches the other side effortlessly.
Whoever is in a chariot can get no further—
spitting water, he drowns.

Between the Ganges and the Yamuna,
there runs a river:

Submerged in it, the outcaste yogini
effortlessly reaches the other shore.

The Ganges and Yamuna (Jamna) Rivers (which run through Bengal) represent the right and left energy channels in the psychophysical body visualized in meditation, also called the channels of perception and dalliance. The river that runs between the Ganges and Yamuna stands for the central channel, which is the channel of purification.

The yogini (yogini is the feminine form of yogi) symbolizes emptiness and selflessness. The yogini is an "outcaste" in that she is not acceptable to those who are attached to their ingrained ideas of things and their images of themselves. Since ordinary society is based on conventions commonly accepted as true, the mind limited to social training cannot accommodate the insight into the emptiness of absoluteness in worldviews.

The *Sandhinirmocana-sutra* explains the self-limiting nature of this "outcasting" reflex in the course of one of its typically scientific discourses on ultimate truth and its inaccessibility to the conditioned mentality: "Someone in ignorance who clings to the signs of the world because of overwhelming interest in perceptual and cognitive signs thus cannot think of, or assess, or believe in the ultimate nirvana that obliterates all signs so that reification ends."[17]

The "submerging" of the outcaste yogini in the central channel of purification means that the practitioner is not focused on fostering meditative perceptions (right channel), or on dallying with their contents (left channel), but on resolving and clarifying experience (central channel). Thus the yogini reaches the "other shore" of liberation "without effort," disentangled from all mental construction.

Sail on, Gypsy, sail on;
there's been a delay on the way.
At the lotus feet of the true teacher,
you will go again to the city of the Victorious.

In the *Saddharmapundarika-sutra* or Lotus Scripture, one of the greatest treasures of Ekayana (Unitarian) Buddhism, the Buddha teaches that *nirvana,* which apparently had been the goal, is actually just a temporary stopping place, an "illusory citadel," on the way to the complete knowledge and vision of Buddhas.

The *sutra* says that a large number of followers who thought they had already attained the ultimate were offended by this statement and left the Buddha's presence. Others remained, admitting that they now realized they had thought themselves saintly when they were actually just decrepit. These people were now able to learn more advanced and comprehensive teachings from Buddha.

This "schism" is one of the great dramas of Buddhism, illustrating an essential truth about history as well as individual development. The exhortation to "sail on, sail on," here addressed by the singer to herself, echoes the Buddha's inspiration to progress, not allowing oneself to stagnate after reaching the deep quiescence experienced in attaining nirvana and merging with emptiness, as illustrated in the first couplet.

This next step, progressing beyond nirvana, called "stepping forward from the top of the hundred foot pole" in Zen, must be taken with care. Freedom implies responsibility. The "true teacher" is truth teaching; the "lotus" is the awakening of the unified, whole mind; the "feet" are the bases of this awakening, the traces of truth by which enlightenment is guided.

The Victor is another name for Buddha, who has mastered the self and in this sense "conquered the world." The city of the Victor is the realm of enlightened experience. Attainment of enlightenment is sometimes referred to as "arrival," in view of the factual transition from a deluded state to an awakened state; but it is also commonly called "return," in the sense that this enlightenment is considered true normalcy, the true "home" of the human essence. Thus enlightenment may also be called restoration, or reversion; so the inspiration says "you will go again."

The five oars are put down,
a rope is tied to the back of the boat;
With the sky for a pot, I bail water,
so it doesn't get in through the cracks.

The five oars are the "five Tathagatas," the five Dhyani Buddhas or Meditation Buddhas used in visualization meditation, as explained earlier. When the enlightened cognitions associated with these Buddhas have been awakened, the practice of deliberate visualization is relinquished. The means are superseded when the goal is reached; thus it is said that "the five oars are put down."

Awakening is followed by stabilization of the realization. This is symbolized by the "rope tied to the back of the boat." In Zen Buddhism, this process of stabilization and maturation is called "nurturing the embryo of sagehood." Initial realization is likened to an infant, which must be nurtured and protected in order to fulfill its potential of wholesome growth and development.

The actual practice of nurturing and protecting the newly awakened mind is depicted in the second line of this couplet.

Here, "water" symbolizes disturbance by objects, the "sky" stands for inner calmness and emptiness. With this "pot" the "water" of disturbance, that may otherwise "get in" through the "cracks" or gaps in attention, is "bailed out," keeping the mind clear and unruffled.

The moon and sun are the mast
upon which creation is unfurled and wrapped up;
The two courses, left and right, do not appear good;
let one sail on at will.

The moon stands for the worldly thought of enlightenment, the thought of enlightenment arising from understanding the relative nature of the world. The sun stands for the absolute thought of enlightenment, the thought of enlightenment arising from insight into inconceivable absolute reality.

When these two are pictured as points, their connection is pictured as a line; the "unfurling" of creation is contemplation of relative reality, the "wrapping up" of creation is contemplation of absolute reality. Going back and forth, from contemplation of the relative to contemplation of the absolute, and from contemplation of the absolute to contemplation of the relative, is a meditative practice designed to lead to the capacity for poise in the center between these extremes, the so-called Middle Way.

The Middle Way is the path the Buddhist seeks to tread, and it is for this purpose that the contemplation of two levels of truth is practiced. Thus "the two courses, left and right, do not appear good." The practitioner leans neither toward the mundane nor toward the absolute, and is thus able to "sail on at will," free of encumbering bias.

Without a penny, without a dime,
one reaches the other side effortlessly.
Whoever is in a chariot can get no further—
spitting water, he drowns.

In the *Vajracchedika Prajnaparamita-sutra,* Buddha says that he did not acquire anything by complete perfect enlightenment. In one sense, this is understood to mean that the awakening and development of Buddhahood is awakening and development of existing potential, not something added. In another sense, it means that enlightenment cannot manifest or develop in the mind while it is occupied by acquisitiveness, or possessiveness.

Ironically enough, intense effort at religious exercises may, in reality, be a manifestation of greed, disguised as spiritual seeking. Devotion may be nothing more than proprietary sentiment. That is why the unencumbered one "without a penny, without a dime" arrives at the "other shore" of transcendence "without effort," while the superficial one who cleaves to an apparatus as truth itself cannot go beyond its limits or avoid its inevitable failure.

15

SHANTI

On discerning analysis of essence,
the imperceptible cannot be observed.
Whoever goes on a straight path
will never turn back.
From shore to shore,
samsara is not a straight path, you fool!
Little child, don't forget a word—
the royal path is steep!
You find no limit to the depth of the sea
of illusion and delusion:
No boat or raft is seen ahead;
you're mistaken not to ask a guide.
In the trackless expanse of emptiness,
nothing can be seen;
you do not entertain doubt as you go.
Here eight great adepts attain fulfillment,
going on the straight path.
Abandoning both left and right paths,
Shanti speaks succinctly;
The river bank has no weeds, no rough ground—
one may go on the way with eyes closed.

On discerning analysis of essence,
the imperceptible cannot be observed.
Whoever goes on a straight path
will never turn back.

Analytic meditation is one method of arriving at emptiness. There are various ways of practicing this type of meditation, including both linear and nonlinear modes of contemplation.

An example of a method in the linear mode is given in the *Heroic Progress Scripture:* "Examine the nature of earth: in its gross form, it is the gross element earth; in its fine form, it is subtle atoms, even subatomic particles next to nothing. On analysis of the most minute form of matter, it is found to be composed of seven parts; when you go even further to break down subatomic particles, this is real emptiness."

An example of a method in the nonlinear mode is in the Zen *koan* "The Wheelmaker" in the classic collection *No Barrier:* "The original wheelmaker made wheels with a hundred spokes. Suppose you take away both sides and remove the axle; what does this clarify?"[18]

A straight path, in Buddhist terms, is a technical term with more than merely moralistic meaning. The *Scripture Spoken by Vimalakirti* says, "A straightforward mind is a site of enlightenment, because it has no falsehood or artificiality." The special sense of straightforward is "direct," meaning direct perception of truth without subjective distortion. Using the same terminology, the illustrious Sixth Grand Master of Zen said, "If you are purely and wholly straightforward in mind everywhere, whatever you are doing, you do not move from the site of enlightenment, which actually becomes the Pure Land. That is called absorption in one practice."

From shore to shore,
samsara is not a straight path, you fool!
Little child, don't forget a word—
the royal path is steep!

Samsara literally means "revolving," and connotes mundane existence, or the world. In Chinese Buddhism, the term is translated as "revolving," "flowing and revolving," and "birth and death." Later Taoism also borrowed this terminology, without externalizing the imagery. Ch'en Ying-ning, a modern Taoist, explains, "The ocean of birth and death is people's thoughts. Random thoughts come from nowhere in an instant, occurring and passing away, impossible to stop altogether. The occurring of a thought is 'birth,' the passing away of a thought is 'death.' In the space of a single day, we are born and die thousands of times! So 'transmigration' is right in front of us—we don't have to wait until we die to experience it."[19]

From shore to shore, therefore, from birth to death or beginning to end, fluctuating thoughts are not a straight path. The "royal path," or the way to real enlightenment, cannot be pursued willy-nilly; to attain right orientation it is necessary to get over the obstacles to understanding created by our mental habits, and perceive reality directly.

You find no limit to the depth of the sea
of illusion and delusion:

No boat or raft is seen ahead;
you're mistaken not to ask a guide.

The apparent objectivity of the perceived "world" as constructed by our brains for navigational purposes is an illusion; the notion that this and nothing else is real or true is a delusion. We find no limit to their depths because the contents of illusion and delusion are self-contained and self-conditioned; the eye of illusion sees only illusions, the eye of delusion sees only delusions. This is encapsulated in the Zen proverb, "When Mr. Chang drinks wine, Mr. Lee gets drunk."

This is the reason for guidance. Even if someone wants to get over illusion and delusion, subjectivity still blinds the mind wrapped up in preconceptions, expectations, hopes, and fears. The possibility of seeing a viable way out is affected by the mental conditioning and emotional state. Thus it is a mistake—indeed, the very same mistake as the original delusion—to rely on what is found through a search based on subjective supposition, without seeking perspective from an objective source of perception and knowledge.

In the trackless expanse of emptiness,
nothing can be seen;
you do not entertain doubt as you go.
Here eight great adepts attain fulfillment,
going on the straight path.

In the *Madhyamika-karika,* Nagarjuna explains that according to the Buddhist usage, "emptiness" means departure, or detachment, from all views. He adds that the Buddhas have also said that those who take emptiness for a view are incurable. Therefore the statement "nothing can be seen" is not a description or a prescription but a test. The orthodox usage means that there is no reification, whereas the deteriorated understanding is literal.

The teaching of Buddhist Yoga states that it is in fact possible to cultivate a state of mind in which no objects appear. This is not regarded as a true state per se, but as a demonstration of a kind of relativity. There are technical terms for this state, and in orthodox schools it is always rigorously distinguished from emptiness. The objectless state is *empty,* in Buddhist terms, but it is not *emptiness.* Those who understand this distinction both intellectually and experientially are capable of further progress.

Pragmatic dimensions of emptiness are expounded in different ways throughout the Buddhist canon. The image of tracklessness appears in the ancient *Dhammapada,* in the section on the Arhat, or Worthy, where Buddha says, "Those whose compulsions are gone, who are not addicted to consuming, whose sphere is emptiness, signlessness, and liberation, are hard to track, like birds in the sky."[20]

Similar imagery and practice were also taught in Zen Buddhism. The 17th-century Japanese master Shigetsu said, "First getting rid of clinging to ego even in the midst of energy and matter, you attain our original state of egolessness. Then you must also know that phenomena have no selfhood either. Once you realize there is no self in persons or things, then you walk in emptiness even in the midst of your daily activities. This is called traveling the bird's path."

The symbolism of the "eight great adepts" who attain fulfillment in this way can refer to the eight consciousnesses or the eight awakenings of great people.

The eight consciousnesses are composed of five sense consciousnesses, the cognitive consciousness *(manovijnana);* the intellect/mentality *(manas),* which includes emotion and judgment; and the "repository" consciousness *(alayavijnana),* in actuality largely subconscious, where all sorts of inherited, experienced, and generated data are stored. The practice of nonreification—departure from all views, or emptiness—purifies the total apparatus of the "eight consciousnesses" of stultifying accumulations of clinging habit.

The eight awakenings of great people are related to this idea, as means of clarification of consciousness and attainment of nirvana. First is having few desires. Buddha said, "People with many desires seek to gain a lot, and therefore their afflictions are also manifold. Those with few desires neither seek nor crave, so they do not have these problems. You should cultivate having few desires even for this reason alone, to say nothing of the fact that having few desires can produce virtues. People with few desires are innocent of using flattery and deviousness to curry the favor of others, and they are not under the compulsion of their senses. Those who act with few desires are calm, without anxiety or fear. Whatever the situation, there is more than enough—there is never insufficiency. Those who have few desires have nirvana."

Second is being content. Buddha said, "If you want to shed afflictions, be content. Contentment is the abode of prosperity and happiness, of peace and serenity."

Third is enjoying quietude. Buddha said, "If you wish to seek the peace and happiness of quietude and noncontrivance, leave the clamor and live an uncluttered life in an uncrowded place. . . . Those who like crowds suffer the vexations of crowds, just as a big tree will suffer withering and breakage when flocks of birds gather on it. Worldly ties and clinging sink you into a multitude of pains, like an old elephant stuck in the mud unable to get itself out."

Fourth is diligence. Buddha said, "Nothing is difficult if you make diligent effort, so you should be diligent. Even a small stream can go through rock if it flows continually."

Fifth is unfailing recollection, or keeping right-mindfulness. Buddha said, "If you seek a good companion, if you seek a good protector and helper, nothing compares to unfailing recollection. Those who have unfailing recollection cannot be invaded by draining afflictions, so you should concentrate your thoughts and keep mindful. One who loses mindfulness loses virtue. If one's power of mindfulness is strong, one will not be harmed even if one enters among draining desires."

Sixth is concentration in meditation. Buddha said, "If you concentrate the mind, it will be in a state of stability, and you will be able to discern the characteristics of phenomena that come to be and pass away in the world."

Seventh is cultivating insight. Buddha said, "If you have insight, you will have no greedy attachment. Always examine yourselves and do not allow any heedlessness. Then you will be able to attain liberation from ego and objects. . . . Genuine insight is a secure ship to cross the sea of aging, ailing, and dying. It is a bright lamp in the darkness of ignorance, it is good medicine for the unwell, and it is a sharp axe to fell the trees of afflictions. So you should use the insight gained by learning, reflection, and application, and develop it in yourself. Anyone who has the illumination of wisdom is a person with clear eyes, even the mortal eyes."

Eighth is not engaging in vain talk. Buddha said, "If you indulge in various kinds of vain talk, your mind will be disturbed. Then you will not attain liberation even if you leave society. Therefore you should immediately give up vain talk, which disturbs the mind. If you want to attain the bliss of tranquillity and dispassion, you should extinguish the affliction of vain talk."

Buddha is said to have articulated these eight awarenesses on the night he passed away into final extinction. According to this tradition, in his last reminder to his followers he said, "Always seek the path of emancipation with a single mind. All things in the world, mobile and immobile, are unstable forms that disintegrate."

Each of these eight awarenesses contains the other; so their integrated awakening is also represented by the number sixty-four. Sixty-four has already appeared in these songs; it stands for the totality of the eight awarenesses in Hinayana Buddhism, the totality of worldly arts and sciences in Mahayana Buddhism, and the totality of erotic arts in Vajrayana Buddhism.

Hinayana Buddhism deals with transcendence, Mahayana deals with nonduality, and Vajrayana deals with creativity. Thus the three phases of Buddhism are interrelated in an orderly continuity. These are all in the realm of relative means, nevertheless, and not absolute ends; so the seeker is warned not to "entertain doubt," not to linger or dally, neither grasping nor rejecting, on the journey through the traceless void.

Abandoning both left and right paths,
Shanti speaks succinctly;
The river bank has no weeds, no rough ground—
one may go on the way with eyes closed.

Graduating from exercises in perception and dalliance, entering into clarity, one attains lucidity and directness. On the "other shore" beyond the stream of confusing thoughts and feelings, clarity is spontaneous, and its growth is natural, with no need of artificial cultivation.

This stage is captured in a Chinese Zen poem composed around the same time as the Bengali song:

Now, when study's complete, it is like before.
When even the finest thread is shed,
then you reach unknowing.
let it be short, let it be long—stop cutting and patching;
Whether it's high or whether it's low, it will level itself.
The abundance or scarcity of the house
is used according to occasion;
roaming serenely in the land,
one goes where his feet take him.

In the *Dhammapada,* Buddha says of this stage, "By what track can you lead the trackless one, the enlightened one, with infinite vision, the one whose victory is not overturned, whose victory none in the world can approach? By what track can you lead the trackless one, the enlightened one, with infinite vision, whom no ensnaring craving can carry away?"[21]

This couplet can also be interpreted from the standpoint of the sudden method, which nevertheless does not contradict the gradualist interpretation. The sudden or immediate method of practice in Sanskrit Tantric tradition is *Mahamudra* or Great Symbol meditation, which resembles a type of Zen meditation.

The Yuan dynasty Zen master Yuansou gives a fairly typical version of this mode of practice: "Real Zennists set a single eye on the state before the embryo is formed, before any signs become distinct. This opens up and clears the mind so that it penetrates the whole universe. . . . Now there is nothing in the universe, nothing mundane or transmundane, to be an object, an opposite, a barrier, or an impediment to you."[22]

The Sung dynasty master Yuan-wu said, "The penetrating spiritual light and vast open tranquility have never been interrupted since beginningless time. The pure, uncontrived, ineffable complete true mind does not act as a partner to objects of material sense, and is not a companion of myriad things."[23]

16

MAHIDHARA

In three bursts,
the black cloud of mystic sound rumbles;
Hearing it,
the fearsome devil and all his cohorts flee.
Intoxicated, the elephant of mind runs;
In thirst, it churns the endless sky.
Sin and virtue both torn away,
the chain is broken from the tethering post.
Urged on by the sky,
the mind has entered nirvana.
Drunk on ambrosia,
one ignores the whole triple world;
To the master of the five objects,
there's no opposition to be seen.
The heat of the rays of the scorching sun
pervade the courtyard of space;
Mahidhara says, "Submerged herein,
nothing do I see."

In three bursts,
the black cloud of mystic sound rumbles;
Hearing it,
the fearsome devil and all his cohorts flee.

The classical Zen master Pai-chang explained the three stages of Buddhism in these terms: "The words of the Teachings all have three successive steps; elementary, intermediate, and final good. . . . The elementary good is teaching that the immediate mirroring awareness is your own Buddha. The intermediate good is not to keep dwelling in the immediate mirroring awareness. The final good is not to make an understanding of nondwelling either."

Pai-chang also expounds this three-step process in greater detail: "When you no longer have clinging attachment, and yet you dwell in nonattachment, considering that correct, this is the elementary good. This is abiding in the subdued mind. . . .

"Once you are no longer grasping and clinging, and yet you do not dwell in nonattachment either, this is the intermediate good. This is the Half Word Teaching. This is still the formless realm; though you avoid falling into the ways of escapists and maniacs, this is still a meditation sickness. . . .

"When you no longer dwell on nonattachment, and do not even make an understanding of not dwelling either, this is the final good. This is the Full Word Teaching. You avoid getting stuck in the formless realm, you avoid lapsing into meditation sickness, you avoid getting stuck in the way of bodhisattvas, and you avoid falling into the state of the king of demons."

Tao-hsin, the Fourth Grand Master of Zen in China, explained the three stages of realization in this manner: "A bodhisattva in the beginning stage first realizes that all is empty. After that, one realizes that all is not empty. This is nondiscriminatory insight. This is the meaning of 'form itself is emptiness.' It is not an emptiness that is the result of annihilation of form; the very nature of form is empty.

"Bodhisattva practice has emptiness as its realization. When beginning learners see emptiness, this is seeing emptiness, not real emptiness. Those who cultivate enlightenment to the point where they attain real emptiness do not see emptiness or nonemptiness; they have no views."

Intoxicated, the elephant of mind runs;
In thirst, it churns the endless sky.

This couplet may have three levels of interpretation. On the ordinary level, referring to the deluded state, it represents the mind besotted by imagination and desire. Impulsive and hasty, this mad mind confuses all clarity.

On the level of confusion seeking enlightenment, these lines represent an abnormal state of excitement. In classical Zen, the "leakage of words" happens when the marvel is spoken so clearly that the unripe intellect loses sight of process. In thirst for attainment of a bewilderingly attractive prospect, the immature mind creates more confusion by subjective desire and consequent haste.

On the level of awakening, this couplet is interpreted to represent the mind ecstatic from the effect of the teaching becoming oblivious to superficial discriminations, soaring untrammeled into the infinity of blissful consciousness beyond the structures of mundane habits of thought.

Sin and virtue both torn away,
the chain is broken from the tethering post.

Urged on by the sky,
the mind has entered nirvana.

A classical Buddhist joke, which nevertheless has a most serious point, says that the true ignoramus is one who hears of transcending good and bad and thinks that means it is good to be bad. Stupid as it may seem when presented in this way, the idea that liberation from "sin and virtue" means license and abandon remains subconsciously in the minds of people trained to think in these terms, even if they have intellectually rejected some or all of the norms according to which they were socialized.

In Buddhist terms, the point where "sin and virtue" are "both torn away" is when the individual is mature enough not to need threats and promises to act with conscience. This is not a rejection of social or moral values; it is the development of a real conscience, based on consciousness rather than indoctrination. No longer chained to an internalized external system of automated response (which is subject to breakdown under conditions of contradiction and other forms of duress and distress), one is now able to act on reality instead of ideology.

The extinction of confusion in nirvana is referred to in Buddhist Yoga as the highest expedient. It is this experience that clears the mind in the way that enables one to come face to face with truth and reality in a direct relationship inaccessible to doctrine, imagination, or intellectual speculation. The irony of nirvana is that while one may be inspired to seek it through fear and hope, or aversion and desire, ultimately nirvana cannot be attained as long as one remains within the domain of fear and hope and aversion and desire.

That is why the song says that the mind has entered nirvana "urged on by the sky," for nirvana is truly attained through actual realization of emptiness, symbolized by the sky, which contains all things without being stained by them.

Drunk on ambrosia,
one ignores the whole triple world;
To the master of the five objects,
there's no opposition to be seen.

Ambrosia means nirvana; drunkenness means detachment from thought. The triple world refers to the realm of desire, the realm of form, and the formless realm. Ignoring the whole triple world is not literal, as drunkenness is not literal; it means being unattached, aloof from all objects in the three realms.

This aloofness and nonattachment does not imply negation or suppression of experience. As the song says, "To the master of the five objects, there's no opposition to be seen." The five objects are objects of the five senses. When the mind is not subject to their influence, there is no need to oppose the senses to be free. The classical Zen master Kuei-shan said, "As long as feelings do not stick to things, how can things hinder you?"

This couplet can be interpreted to represent the spiritual "death and rebirth" process of liberating the mind from worldly influences by "ignoring" the whole world in nirvanic "drunkenness," and then, after that, returning to the world with self-mastery to secure the freedom of mind in the midst of worldly things.

This process is illustrated in the story of a wayfarer who went to a Zen master and said, "Who is not a companion of myriad things?" The master said, "I'll tell you when you can swallow the water of the West River in one gulp." At this the wayfarer attained enlightenment.

The Zen exercise of "not being a companion of myriad things" is a practical equivalent of the Tantric "drunk on ambrosia, ignoring the whole triple world." The Zen awakening of the immediate mirroring awareness, "swallowing the water of the river in one gulp," is the experiential equivalent of the Tantric "mastery of the five objects, without opposition to be seen."

The heat of the rays of the scorching sun
pervade the courtyard of space;
Mahidhara says, "Submerged herein,
nothing do I see."

The sun is enlightened consciousness, the heat of its rays is the certitude of enlightened insight, evaporating the mists of illusion. The courtyard of space is emblematic of the vastness of the enlightened perspective, the pervasion of the sunlight represents the completeness and comprehensiveness of enlightened perception.

Zen master Yuan-wu wrote, "The penetrating spiritual light and vast open tranquility have always been there. The pure, uncontrived, ineffable, complete true mind does not act as a partner to objects of material sense, and is not a companion of myriad things. When the mind is always as clear and bright as ten suns shining together, detached from views and beyond feelings, cutting through the ephemeral illusions of birth and death, this is what is meant by the saying 'Mind itself is Buddha.'"[24]

17

VINA

The moon is joined to the gourd of the sun,
making a mandolin;
The ascetic has fashioned
an unstrummed stem and disc.
Play, friend, the lyre of Heruka;
The sound of the strings of emptiness,
compassion does enjoy.
Contemplating the arrays of vowels and consonants,
The supreme elephant
equanimously awaits an opening.
When the edge of the palm
presses the instrument's spring,
The notes of the thirty-two strings all emanate.
The Thunderbolt Bearer dances, the Goddess sings;
The Buddha-drama is unparalleled.

The moon is joined to the gourd of the sun,
making a mandolin;
The ascetic has fashioned
an unstrummed stem and disc.

The moon, the relative thought of enlightenment, is joined to the sun, the absolute thought of enlightenment, making an instrument of awakening. The ascetic also means the central channel of the psychic nerve system, the channel of purification. It is the process of purification that joins the sun and moon, the relative and absolute thought of enlightenment. Centered and cleared, awakened consciousness is not caused to vibrate, or resonate, by external impacts; so the instrument is "unstrummed."

Play, friend, the lyre of Heruka;
The sound of the strings of emptiness,
compassion does enjoy.

Heruka is a symbolic personification of the Dharma or reality that underlies the teaching. The reality and the teaching it engenders are summarized in emptiness and compassion. The Heruka is a "wrathful" form, representing active destruction of ignorance, the liberative quality of the compassion of emptiness.

Liberative compassion is realized through emptiness, for it is by the experience and realization of emptiness that compassion is enabled to rise above sentimentality. Sentimental compassion is intrinsically limited and limiting. Emptiness is not realized in nihilism or cynicism but rather in fluidity and openness. Thus, the experiential realization of emptiness makes it possible to perceive and express objective, impartial compassion.

Contemplating the arrays of vowels and consonants,
The supreme elephant
equanimously awaits an opening.

Discerning the structure of the world of conventionally conditioned vision and understanding as reflected in routine habits of thought, the self-possessed mind calmly watches for the gaps, through which other dimensions of reality can be perceived and employed.

When the edge of the palm
presses the instrument's string,
The notes of the thirty-two strings all emanate.

According to the teaching of the *Lotus* scripture, thirty-two is the number of manifestations of Avalokitesvara, the multi-faceted personification of compassion, whose name literally means "the power of objective observation."

The capacity to project different personalities in compassionate response to situational needs is a characteristic of the *bodhisattva,* who has taken autonomous control of the mind-body instrument.

The number thirty-two also refers, in the context of Tantric Buddhism, to the network of energy channels visualized in the body of spiritual experience. This network is conceived of as an internal counterpart to thirty-two marks of distinction on the idealized external image of a Buddha. Interpreted in this sense, the couplet refers to the activation of the energy network after the mind has been cleared by going through the "opening" in the "vowels and consonants" of conceptual thought.

The Thunderbolt Bearer dances, the Goddess sings;
The Buddha-drama is unparalleled.

The Thunderbolt Bearer represents the created universe, expedient means, and structured knowledge; the body, speech, and mind of the cosmic Buddha in its manifest aspect. The Goddess represents space, formless insight, and emptiness; the body, speech, and mind of the cosmic Buddha in its occult aspect.

The Buddha-drama of the interplay of the Thunderbolt Bearer and the Goddess is "unparalleled" because it features the entire cosmos, abstract and concrete, in its all-inclusive cast. The mind of the practitioner absorbed in this drama becomes merged, imbued, and identified with the cosmic realities of Buddhahood.

18

KRISHNAVAJRA

I traverse the three realms without effort;
I sleep in the play of great bliss.
No matter what your conduct, Gypsy woman,
You're a ragged mendicant
in the midst of respectable people.
Everything is destroyed by you, Gypsy woman!
Work left undone, the moon is eclipsed.
Some people may call you ugly,
But the wise never leave you.
Krishna sings, "You act the outcaste woman;
There is no immoral woman better than the Gypsy!"

I traverse the three realms without effort;
I sleep in the play of great bliss.

The "three realms" are the realm of desire, the realm of form, and the realm of formless abstraction. These include all possible mundane and heavenly states of mind. "Traversing" means not dwelling, recognizing that one is a temporary traveler in this world, not a permanent resident. "Without effort" means free from artificiality, without contrivance.

"Sleep" stands for detachment from the images of the world, "great bliss" for the serene spiritual transport this detachment engenders. "Play" represents the experience of life without the burden of self-importance.

No matter what your conduct, Gypsy woman,
You're a ragged mendicant
in the midst of respectable people.

The *Hrdaya-sutra* or *Heart Scripture* says, "Form is not different from emptiness, emptiness is not different from form; form is itself emptiness, emptiness is itself form." The "conduct" of the "gypsy woman" is the form of emptiness; in whatever form emptiness appears, it is still emptiness. The "respectable people" are the outward forms of the known world; the "ragged mendicant" is the inner essence that is beyond the reach of conceptualization.

Everything is destroyed by you, Gypsy woman!
Work left undone, the moon is eclipsed.

As Nagarjuna wrote, "Emptiness is departure from all views." What is "destroyed" by the "gypsy woman" of emptiness is the sense of ixity and absoluteness that seems like a characteristic of the external world. Seen in reality as a characteristic of subjective habit, assumption, and conditioning, this illusion of absoluteness is thereby "destroyed."

In the religious field, Munidatta defines the "gypsy woman" of emptiness as *asampradaya,* which can mean nonsectarian, or not having an established doctrine, traditional belief, or usage. This is "departure from all views," in recognition of the fact that established doctrines, traditional beliefs, and customary usages are locally and temporally conditioned phenomena, not timeless absolutes; and therefore of relatively local, temporal, and conditional worth, not absolute, unqualified value.

According to the *Sandhinirmocana-sutra,* the classic textbook of Buddhist Yoga, those who see the absolute truth "can and do dismiss the forms of practices," and they "can and do shed bondage to forms." This is the sense of the expression "work left undone." According to the *Flower Ornament Scripture,* "As soon as they attain the eighth stage, Immovability, enlightening beings become freed from all efforts and attain the state of effortlessness, freed from physical, verbal, and mental striving, freed from stirring cogitation and flowing thoughts, and become stabilized in a natural state of development."

The "moon," as the mundane or relative thought of enlightenment, serves to orient the intellectual and emotional faculties toward enlightenment in the "dark night of ignorance," that is, even while still in the realm of ordinary conventional conditioning. As such, it may involve attraction and aversion, both intellectual and emotional. When the absolute thought of enlightenment is subequently awakened by the experience of emptiness, its direct, unmediated authenticity "eclipses" the moon of relative understanding.

Some people may call you ugly,
But the wise never leave you.

When people fear or reject the teaching of emptiness, they usually are thinking of it in a nihilistic way, or they feel their imaginary self, personal predilections, and subjective biases are being threatened. There is no real comparison, however, accessible to the mind wrapped up in its own subjectivity, as the *Sandhinirmocana-sutra* explains: "A man accustomed to pungent and bitter flavors all his life cannot think of, or assess, or believe in the sweet taste of honey and sugar. Someone in ignorance who has an overwhelming interest in desires because of passionate craving, and is therefore inflamed with excitement, thus cannot think of, or assess, or believe in the marvelous bliss of detachment and inward effacement of all sense data."

Krishna sings, "You act the outcaste woman;
There is no immoral woman better than the Gypsy!"

Emptiness is "outcaste" in that it does not fit into conventional thinking; it is a "woman" in being pregnant with all things. The nature of emptiness is not "immoral" in the relative sense of being "unconventional," but in the absolute sense of being nonconventional, or inconceivable.

This is why the bliss of realization is called "spontaneous" or "natural." It is not just an exaggerated state induced by concentration. As a classical Zen master Lin-chi said, citing an even more ancient maxim, "Even if there were something beyond nirvana, I would say it is like a dream, or an illusion."

19

KRISHNA

Being and nirvana—tabor and drum.
Mind and breath—rattle and cymbal.
Hail, hail! The drum is sounded!
Krishna's going to marry the Gypsy!
Getting married, the Gypsy devours birth;
Her dowry consists of unexcelled truth.
Day and night are passed in lovemaking;
The night is spent among yoginis.

Being and nirvana—tabor and drum.
Mind and breath—rattle and cymbal.

Return to the Source, a famous contemplative treatise by Fa tsang, one of the main expositors of Hua-yen or Flower Ornament Buddhism, expresses the normative doctrine of the nonduality of being and nirvana in these terms: "In ultimate truth, things are empty and quiescent in their fundamental nature; in conventional truth, things seem to exist yet are empty. The ultimate and conventional, purely empty, are null and groundless."[25]

This is a pattern for contemplation of the integration of being and nirvana, of the relative and the absolute. The treatise goes on to define the pragmatic experience of this contemplation further: "Once relating cognition is stilled, objects related to are empty. Mind and objects not constraining, essence pervades, empty and open."

The second line of the Bengali couplet follows up with a method of stilling the discriminatory mind to perceive the nonduality of being and nirvana. This is summed up in the relationship of mind and breath. *The Secret of the Golden Flower,* a Zen Taoist compendium of meditation methods, says, "The breath is one's own mind; one's own mind does the breathing. Once mind stirs, then there is energy. Energy is basically an emanation of mind. Our thoughts are very rapid; a single random thought takes place in a moment, whereupon an exhalation and inhalation respond to it. Therefore inner breathing and outer breathing accompany each other like sound and echo. In one single day you breathe countless times, so you have countless random thoughts. When the luminosity of spirit has leaked away completely, you are like a withered tree, like dead ashes.

"So should you have no thoughts? It is impossible to have no thoughts. Should you not breathe? It is impossible not to breathe. Nothing compares to making the affliction itself into medicine, which means to have mind and breath rest on each other."[26]

Hail, hail! The drum is sounded!
Krishna's going to marry the Gypsy!

Buddhist teaching is commonly symbolized as a drum in scripture. In particular, the drum's characteristics of inner hollowness with outer responsiveness represent emptiness. Since the point of the teaching is realization of emptiness, here the Tantric adept Krishna presents the image of the drum as signaling marriage with "the Gypsy," or union with emptiness.

Getting married, the Gypsy devours birth;
Her dowry consists of unexcelled truth.

Birthlessness, or nonorigination, is one of the most important technical terms of universalist Buddhism. The attainment of the stage of immovability and nonregression is said to be contingent upon realization of the "birthlessness" or "nonorigination" of all phenomena, graphically represented here as the "Gypsy devouring birth."

The *Sandhinirmocana-sutra* explains this elusive perception in these terms: "What is the essencelessness of the birth of things? It is the dependently originated character of things. Why? Because they exist dependent on the power of other conditions and do not exist of themselves. This is called essencelessness of birth."

The "dowry of unexcelled truth," or realization of the absolute truth, is also defined more explicitly in the same *sutra:* Buddha says, "I also allude to ultimate essencelessness revealed by the selflessness of things when I say that all things have no origination or extinction and are fundamentally quiescent and inherently nirvanic. This is because the ultimate essencelessness revealed by the selflessness of things is the eternal and constant real nature of all things, permanent and uncreated, having no relation to any defilements."[27]

Day and night are passed in lovemaking;
The night is spent among yoginis.

Lovemaking day and night represents constant intercourse with emptiness, both rationally (day) and intuitively (night). Spending the night among yoginis (female yogis) represents intimacy with subtle mystical insights and epiphanies in the extraordinary ranges of consciousness accessible to the opened mind.

Whoever is devoted to the Gypsy woman
Will not let go for a moment,
intoxicated with naturalness.

Someone asked an ancient Zen master, "What about when someone who has realized enlightenment returns to confusion?" The Zen master replied, "A broken mirror does not shine again; fallen leaves do not return to the branches." Someone who is "devoted to the Gypsy woman," someone who has realized emptiness and is free from the bondage of rigid views and absolutist thinking, can no longer be deluded by illusion. Sloughing off restricted habits of thought implanted by conditioning and accident, the mind regains its natural spontaneity, expansive and buoyant, unencumbered by artificialities.

20

KUKKURI

I am without hope, an ascetic husband;
My pleasure cannot be told.
It's opened up, O Mother,
the confinement room's been found;
The one I look for here is not here at all.
The first conception is of the seeds of our desires;
Examining the arteries, attend the phantom shape.
When our youth is fulfilled,
We're uprooted and collected to our fathers.
Kukkuri says, "This world is quiet;
Who awakes here is a hero."

I am without hope, an ascetic husband;
My pleasure cannot be told.

Zen is based on enlightenment, but a cardinal rule of Zen is not to anticipate enlightenment. The reason for this approach is that the anticipation contains subjective wishes, desires, and imaginations, which impede the clarification of the mind. Therefore, as Kukkuri says in the first line of this couplet, the ascetic practice of one who would mate with emptiness lies in entertaining no hope, even while acting in a purposeful manner.

This is much more difficult than torturing oneself in expectation of transcendental rewards. The difficulty is not that of gross hardship, but of subtlety and balance. Being without hope in this sense does not mean cynicism or despair; it is a sort of waiting without anticipation. Because the experience of emptiness is literally inconceivable, the spiritual transport engendered cannot be described in terms of ordinary sensation or feeling; hence the "pleasure cannot be told."

It's opened up, O Mother,
the confinement room's been found;
The one I look for here is not here at all.

The mother stands for egolessness, the confinement room is the innermost mind. When the essence of mind is known as it is, the self as ordinarily conceived or imagined is not there. That secondary, acquired self is not the natural essence of mind, but is composed of conditions, habits, and products of mind.

This couplet represents the practice known in Zen and neoTaoism as "turning the light around." The syncretic Zen Taoist meditation text called *The Secret of the Golden Flower* says, "If you can look back again and again into the source of mind, whatever you are doing, not sticking to any image of person or self, then this is 'turning the light around wherever you are.' This is the finest practice."[28]

The first conception is of the seeds of our desires;
Examining the arteries, attend the phantom shape.

The first conception refers to the physical body; the phantom shape is the psychic or energetic body, which is engendered by concentration and visualization. The arteries are the psychic energy channels used to structure visualization. *The Secret of the Golden Flower* says, "What is most wondrous is when the light has crystallized in a spiritual body, gradually becoming consciously effective."[29] Attending the phantom shape is taught in the aftermath of emptiness realization, to go beyond the "great death" of nirvana without coming back to gross materialism.

When our youth is fulfilled,
We're uprooted and collected to our fathers.

On the ordinary level, this recollection fortifies the resolution to learn how to shift attention from the relative to the absolute, and how to shift energy from the physical body to the psychic body.

The 13th-century Japanese Zen master Dogen said, "Students should think of the fact that they will surely die. This truth is indisputable. But even if you do not think about that fact, for the time being you should at least determine not to pass the time in vain."

The Secret of the Golden Flower says, "From the point of view of the universe, human beings are like mayflies. From the point of view of the Way, even the universe is as an evanescent reflection."[30]

On the literal level, therefore, this couplet refers to the state of cause of practice. On the symbolic level, however, it refers to the state of effect of practice. When immaturity is ended, naive realism and overweening self-importance are shed, illusions are undermined, and perennial truth is seen.

Kukkuri says, "This world is quiet;
Who awakes here is a hero."

The traditional order of Buddhist practice is to realize the emptiness of person first, then to realize the emptiness of phenomena after that. The word "quiet," when it is used in an overtly nonobjective sense, is sometimes employed to express the subjective experience of someone in a state of profound abstraction. More often it is used to express the underlying emptiness of all things, to emphasize the fact that the clamor of the world is created, and to represent inner perception of "leisure within hurry," the absolute within the relative.

In simple terms, the critical point to see and reflect upon is the practical fact that the world itself is not our confusion, or the source of our confusion; we ourselves create the confusion in our relationship with the world. We then become locked into this confusion when we relate to our relationship with the world as if it were the world itself.

The meaning of seemingly arcane Buddhist expressions like "nondoing," "noncontrivance," and "nonreification" becomes clear in this context, when it is realized that the shackles of stultifying routine, needing repetition for cohesion, can therefore be "undone" by being "nondone."

21

BHUSUKU

In the dark of night, the mouse is about;
It eats nectar—the mouse gathers food.
Kill, O yogi, the pilfering mouse,
So that its comings and goings break off.
Digging into the world, the mouse digs a well;
The restless mouse knows it exists for destruction.
The black mouse knows no direction;
Mental reality travels the sky.
Then the mouse is restless;
The true teacher's enlightenment will quiet it down.
When the mouse's scurrying is cut off,
Bhusuku says that bondage ends then.

In the dark of night, the mouse is about;
It eats nectar—the mouse gathers food.

In the midst of activity, the mind is influenced, and taxed, not only by the environment, but also by subtle, subconscious streams of thought and feeling scurrying around in the back of the mind, affecting perceptions, reactions, and patterns of energy flow unawares. This subliminal activity is usually only noticed in attentive stillness.

Kill, O yogi, the pilfering mouse,
So that its comings and goings break off.

Zen master Hung-chih said, "If you want to be even-minded and peaceful, you must put an end to the subtle pounding and weaving in the mind. Do you want to not grumble? You must cut if off and cast it down. Then you can see through it all."

Digging into the world, the mouse digs a well;
The restless mouse knows it exists for destruction.

When it becomes consciously aware of its own instability and ultimate transience, the fluctuating mind itself generates the relative thought of enlightenment.

The black mouse knows no direction;
Mental reality travels the sky.

Unenlightened thought does not correspond to objective conditions; mental reality is projected in the vacuum between subject and object.

Then the mouse is restless;
The true teacher's enlightenment will quiet it down.

Were thought and feeling actually linked to objective reality, there would be no uncertainty. As long as thought and feeling continuously feed themselves and each other, and also feed on themselves and each other, in self-conditioning closed-circuit channels, there is ongoing unrest. Indeed, because the entire process is one of self-reflection, cessation of the routine is felt, and feared, as a threat of annihilation. Only by authentic enlightenment, seeing through the vanity of self-reflection and attaining to truthfulness of self-understanding, is it possible to experience the genuine repose of naturalness.

When the mouse's scurrying is cut off,
Bhusuku says that bondage ends then.

In the *Dhammapada,* Buddha says, "Knowing the extinction of conditioning, you know the uncreated."[31] Zen master Hungchih said, "When your state is thoroughly peaceful and your life is cool and serene, then you will see the emptiness of the ages, where there is nothing to be troubled with, nothing that can obstruct you."

22

SARAHA

One constructs being and nirvana by oneself;
In vain do people fetter themselves.
I don't know the inconceivable yogi;
How can birth and death exist?
Where there is birth, there is death;
Living and dying have no difference.
Whoever is apprehensive of birth and death here
Should desire the rejuvenating elixir.
Whoever roams the universe, even the heavens
Never becomes free of old age and death.
Whether action's caused by birth, or birth by
action, Saraha says, the Truth is inconceivable.

One constructs being and nirvana by oneself;
In vain do people fetter themselves.

Buddha said, "It is by oneself that evil is done, it is by oneself that one is afflicted. It is by oneself that evil is not done, it is by oneself that one is purified. Purity and impurity are individual matters; no one purifies another."[32]

I don't know the inconceivable yogi;
How can birth and death exist?

The emperor of China asked the founder of Zen, "What is the ultimate meaning of the holy truths?" The Zen founder replied, "Empty, nothing holy." The emperor asked, "Who are you?" The Zen founder replied, "I don't know."

The "inconceivable yogi" is the Buddha-nature, or true self, which is not the socially conditioned personality, or the idea of self or image of the ego. Because this nature is not identical to the subjective stream of consciousness, it does not come and go.

Where there is birth, there is death;
Living and dying have no difference.

Whatever is born must die; this is the nature of transitory existence. Buddhists therefore seek liberation from psychological subjection to impermanent things. According to the *Dhammapada,* Buddha said, "What attachment is there when one has seen these white bones as like gourds discarded in autumn?"[33]

Whoever is apprehensive of birth and death here
Should desire the rejuvenating elixir.

The Sufi master Hadrat Ali said, "The world is a transitory abode, not a permanent abode. And the people in it are of two sorts: one who sells his soul and ruins it; and one who ransoms his soul and frees it."[34] Buddha said, "What mirth is there, what joy, while constantly burning? Shrouded in darkness, why not seek a light?"[35]

Whoever roams the universe, even the heavens
Never becomes free of old age and death.

Buddha said, "There is nowhere in the world—not in the sky, nor in the sea, nor in the depths of the earth—where death will not overcome you."[36] The Sufi master Ali said, "Whoever capitulates to the perishing of this world and the next perishes in them."[37]

Whether action's caused by birth, or birth by action, Saraha says, the Truth is inconceivable.

The *Flower Ornament Scripture* says, "All consequences are born from actions; like dreams, they're not truly real. They continually die away, moment to moment, the same as before and after. Of all things seen in the world, only mind is the host; by grasping forms according to interpretation, it becomes deluded, not true to reality. All philosophies in the world are mental fabrications; there has never been a doctrine by which one could enter the true essence of things."[38]

23

SHANTI

Carding the cotton fiber by fiber,
Card and card the fibers to ultimate isolation.
Even then Heruka is not attained;
Why not contemplate it, Shanti says.
Carding the cotton, I feed it to the void;
With the void, I exhaust myself.
In a multitude of paths, no two ways are to be seen;
Not even a hairtip enters, Shanti says.
Neither action nor agency—the reason for this,
According to Shanti, is self-understanding.

Carding the cotton fiber by fiber,
Card and card the fibers to ultimate isolation.

This couplet refers to analytic meditation. By reducing everything to elements and conditions, the mind is disabused of the illusion of things existing in and of themselves.

Even then Heruka is not attained;
Why not contemplate it, Shanti says.

The experience of emptiness realized by analytic reduction is called "mere emptiness," or "empty emptiness," or "partial emptiness." It is also called "empty thusness." Beyond this is the experience called "nonempty emptiness," or "nonempty thusness." In this way illusion is shattered.

Carding the cotton, I feed it to the void;
With the void, I exhaust myself.

Analytic meditation reduces phenomena to emptiness. Understanding the emptiness of all things, one realizes the emptiness, or ultimate unreality, of the personality and ego structure as conditioned by relating to the world of objects as objective reality itself.

In a multitude of paths, no two ways are to be seen;
Not even a hairtip enters, Shanti says.

The Zen classic known as *The Blue Cliff Record* says, "In one there are many kinds; in two there is no duality." In his popular work *Skeletons,* the medieval Japanese Zen master Ikkyu wrote, "Although there are many paths up the base of the mountain, we see the same moon on the high peak." The enormous diversity of Buddhist teachings and practices is based on the application of the principle of *upaya-kausalya,* or "skill in means," according to which the teaching must be adapted to specific needs. Without suitable adaptation, the essential liberative quality of the teaching is lost; doctrine becomes dogma, training becomes conditioning.

The unity of the end, in contrast to the diversity of the means, is also emphasized in Buddhist Yoga, as explained in the *Sandhinirmocana-sutra:* "The selflessness of phenomena in the ultimate sense in true thusness is not said to have a cause, is not causally produced, is not created. This is ultimate truth. Having realized this ultimate truth, one no longer seeks any other ultimate truth. There is only the stability of the true nature of things, the abiding of the realm of reality, which is constant and perpetual whether or not Buddhas appear in the world."[39]

This scriptural passage also explains Shanti's statement that "not even a hairtip enters." Nothing can be added to the absolute unity of ultimate truth, nothing can divide it. Zen literature says of the absolute that "wind cannot penetrate it, water cannot wet it." The Zen collection *No Barrier* speaks of attuning the mind to ultimate truth in these terms: "Better to let go of everything, from space on, for such subtle secrecy that nothing can get in."

Neither action nor agency—the reason for this, According to Shanti, is self-understanding.

Self-understanding includes understanding the nature and character of mental construction. Only thus is it possible to distinguish subjectivity from objectivity. The *Flower Ornament Scripture* says, "Eye, ear, nose, tongue, body, mind, intellect, senses: by these, one always revolves, yet there is no one and nothing that revolves. The nature of things is fundamentally birthless, yet they appear to have birth; herein there is no revealer, and nothing that's revealed. Eye, ear, nose, tongue, body, mind, intellect, senses: all are void and essenceless, but the deluded mind conceives them to exist. Seen as they truly are, all are without inherent nature. The eye of reality is not conceptual; this seeing is not false. Real or unreal, false or not false, worldly or unworldly—there's nothing but descriptions."[40]

24

BHUSUKU

The lotus blooms at full midnight,
Thirty-two yoginis are thereupon uplifted.
The moon is made to go on the path
of the central channel;
Through the jewel, naturalness is expressed.
The moon goes to nirvana;
The lotus plant conveys its juice through the stalk.
The bliss of cessation is formless and pure;
Whoever realizes this is enlightened.
"I have realized it by union," Bhusuku says,
"In the desire for the great ecstasy of natural bliss."

The lotus blooms at full midnight,
Thirty-two yoginis are thereupon uplifted.

Midnight symbolizes inner silence, the quieting of the internal talk. The same image is also used in Zen Buddhism, and in Taoist inner alchemy. This silence allows room for the blossoming of latent or dormant mental capacity that is otherwise usually drowned out by inner conversation.

In terms of visualization practice, the lotus blossom is commonly used as a pedestal or foundation of imagery evoked for contemplation. The perfection of this visualization only becomes possible on a background of inner silence, for otherwise the mind is too preoccupied, scattered, and distracted to hold an image steady enough for practical use.

In terms of the first-mentioned level of interpretation, the uplifting of the thirty-two yoginis represent the unfolding of spiritual subtleties. In terms of visualization practice, the thirty-two yoginis stand for the system of energy channels and nodes, which can be activated after the perceptual bias of coarse consciousness is stilled in the "midnight" of inner silence.

The moon is made to go on the path
of the central channel;
Through the jewel, naturalness is expressed.

In visualization practice, the moon is placed above the lotus blossom; this stands for the thought of enlightenment. Certain letters or images, containing the meanings that inspire the thought of enlightenment, may also be visualized on the moon. Then the moon is "absorbed" into the body, conveying the sense of internalization of the inspiration. Then the "jewel," the precious essence of mind, now being freed from the dross of worldliness by the thought of enlightenment, is able to express its natural spirituality.

The moon goes to nirvana;
The lotus plant conveys its juice through the stalk.

Abstractly, the moon going to nirvana represents the thought of enlightenment culminating in perfect peace of mind.

Concretely, in visualization practice, this follows on the previous couplet, representing the image of the moon, aglow with the conscious energy of inspiration, rising up the central channel to the node of Nirvana at the center of the crown of the head. The rising of the energy, producing inner bliss, is graphically represented by the rising of the juice through the stalk of the lotus.

Chinese Taoists using visualization systems of energy channels and nodes similar to that used in Tantric Buddhism sometimes refer to the center of the crown as the Nirvana *(Ni-wan)* point, and the center of the brain as the Nirvana Chamber. This latter also corresponds to the preliminary location of the point called Most Hidden *(Akhfaa)* in the Five Subtleties system of the Sufis, who warn against experimentation and make it clear that these are not actual physical locations, but are used as concentration points for purposes of mental orientation.[d]

The bliss of cessation is formless and pure;
Whoever realizes this is enlightened.

The bliss of cessation is the subtle transport of nirvana. The great Sung dynasty Zen master Yuan-wu wrote, "Let go of all your previous imaginings, opinions, interpretations, worldly knowledge, intellectualism, egoism, and competitiveness; become like a dead tree, like cold ashes. When you reach the point where feelings are ended, views are gone, and your mind is clean and naked, you open up to realization."[41]

"I have realized it by union," Bhusuku says,
"In the desire for the great ecstasy of natural bliss."

This yoga, or "union," is also called return to the source. It is a restoration of natural primal unity, rather than a contrived compromise of fundamentally dissident aspects of mind. Because this union is not contrived, it is literally inconceivable; its reality is experienced in the "great ecstasy," or "aloof standpoint" of "teacherless knowledge," direct inner cognition.

This yoga of union with the original buoyancy of the spontaneous natural mind is explained by the celebrated Sung dynasty Zen master Hung-chih in terms of both process and attainment: "When you are open and naturally aware, clean and naturally clear, you are capable of panoramic consciousness without making an effort to grasp perception, and you are capable of discerning understanding without the burden of conditioned thought. You go beyond being and nothingness, and transcend conceivable feelings. This is only experienced by union with it; it is not gotten from another."[42]

25

SHABARA

High, high the mountain;
there dwells a mountain girl,
Wearing peacock feathers
and a necklace of gunja berries.
Mad mountain man, crazy Shabara,
please do not make a ruckus;
Your own wife is called the Beauty of Naturalness.
The mountain girl roams the forest by herself,
A thunderbolt bearer in earrings.
The mountain savage fills the bed of the triple world,
a nice bed covered with great ecstasy.
The savage lover and the selfless consort
pass the night in love.
I chew the betel of mind
with the camphor of great ecstasy;
Taking empty selflessness to heart,
I pass the night in bliss.
The bow of the teacher's words
strikes with the arrow of one's own mind;
With one arrow shot, pierce through,
pierce through to ultimate nirvana.
The savage is maddened with profound rage;
Gone into the clefts of the peaks,
how can the savage be found?

High, high the mountain;
there dwells a mountain girl,
Wearing peacock feathers
and a necklace of gunja berries.

The mountain girl represents *sunyata,* emptiness, and *nairatmya,* selflessness or identitylessness. The mountain and its height stand for transcendence beyond worldly views. Peacock feathers allude to the colors associated with visualization practice. *Gunja,* overtly referring to a type of berry, also means "murmuring" and "meditation," thus alluding to repetition of mantras and meditations. The fact that the girl is "wearing" the feathers and necklace represents the fact that formal practices are still externals, expedient means, not the realization of emptiness itself.

Mad mountain man, crazy Shabara,
please do not make a ruckus;
Your own wife is called the Beauty of Naturalness.

The name of the adept, Shabara, literally means a mountaineer, a barbarian, a savage. This image, especially with the added description of madness and craziness, alludes to what is beyond convention. The mad mountain man is asked not to make a ruckus in the sense that transcendence of convention is not accomplished by destroying convention or trying to be unconventional (postures which are still attached to convention, albeit by opposition), but by realizing the nature of convention as convention and not absolute reality. The inherent emptiness of convention, which means being empty of absoluteness, is symbolized by the mountaineer's own wife, the "beauty of naturalness."

In its natural state, relative reality, in itself, is innocent of the restrictions of conceptualized reality. The *Sandhinirmocanasutra* says. "The ultimate essencelessness revealed by the selflessness of things is the eternal and constant real nature of all things, permanent and uncreated, having no relation to any defilements."[43] So there is no need to "make a ruckus" to be free, for existence and emptiness inherently interpenetrate, already "married" in natural reality.

The mountain girl roams the forest by herself,
A thunderbolt bearer in earrings.

The forest of delusion is inherently empty; this realization itself shatters illusions.

The mountain savage fills the bed of the triple world,
a nice bed covered with great ecstasy.
The savage lover and the selfless consort
pass the night in love.

In Zen terminology, initial realization of emptiness is referred to as "sitting atop a hundred-foot pole." In the classic *No Barrier,* an ancient master is quoted as saying, "Atop a hundred-foot pole, one should step forward to manifest the whole body throughout the universe." It is as though union with emptiness were like cleaning a vast mirror, in which the whole universe is then reflected.

The "great ecstasy" with which the "bed of the triple world" is covered refers to the ethereal nondiscursive consciousness of the mind freed from its prison of conditioned conceptualizations. The mountain savage and the selfless consort passing the night in love represents the oneness of existence and emptiness realized by freeing the mind from the belief in conceptual description as objective reality.

I chew the betel of mind
with the camphor of great ecstasy;
Taking empty selflessness to heart,
I pass the night in bliss.

In Buddhist practice, ecstasy is instrumental; it is not pursued or experienced as an end in itself. A result of cessation of internal talk, it is then used to dissolve the habit of compulsive conceptualization. This enables the practitioner to "take empty selflessness to heart" by direct perception of "the ultimate essencelessness revealed by the selflessness of things," attained by "knowledge that is not conditioned by words, not thinking in conformity with words, free from the lull of words." As before, the "night" represents, from the point of view of practice, the state of mind in which words and concepts are inoperative; and, from the point of view of realization, the ultimate truth to which no words or concepts can actually apply.

The bow of the teacher's words
strikes with the arrow of one's own mind;
With one arrow shot, pierce through,
pierce through to ultimate nirvana.

The instructions of the teacher provide impetus and direction, but it is the mind of the practitioner that must "fly." Along the way there are many obstacles; it is necessary to penetrate them resolutely in order to arrive at the aim.

The savage is maddened with profound rage;
Gone into the clefts of the peaks,
how can the savage be found?

The "profound rage" of the "savage" represents the mental revolution, referred to technically in Sanskrit as *paravrtti,* "turning back" or "recoiling," in which the mind turns away from the illusions of the world to realize transcendence. In *The Blue Cliff Record* , a Zen master says, "With my staff across my shoulder, I pay no heed to people; I go straight into the myriad peaks."

26

LUI

Being does not exist, nonbeing does not work;
Who believes in such an enlightenment?
The Way, Lui says, is inscrutable to conception;
Sporting in the triple world, I cannot be detected.
He to whom color, character,
and figure are not known—
How can he discourse on scriptural knowledge?
You will present me with questions,
"Whose?" "What?"
Like the moon in the water, it is neither real nor false.
Lui says, "As long as I will be,
The one with whom I am will be unseen."

Being does not exist, nonbeing does not work;
Who believes in such an enlightenment?

This couplet expresses the Middle Way. In the Buddhist perspective, "being does not exist" in the specific sense that what exists only conceptually or relatively does not exist absolutely. "Nonbeing," on the other hand, "does not work" because it is inert. The *Sandhinirmocana-sutra* explains the fallacy of a nihilistic interpretation of emptiness: "If people have not yet been able to accumulate stores of superior virtue and knowledge, and are not simple and direct by nature, and still persist in clinging to their own views even though they have the power to think discerningly and to discard and affirm, when they hear such a teaching, they are unable to truly understand what I say with hidden intent. Even if they believe in such a teaching, they make a rigid literal interpretation of the meaning, saying that all things definitely have no essence, definitely are not originated or extinguished, definitely are fundamentally quiescent, and definitely are inherently nirvanic. Because of this, they acquire a view of nothingness, or a view of nonexistence of characteristics, in regard to all things. Because they get the idea of nothingness, or the idea of nonexistence of characteristics, they deny all characteristics, saying they are nonexistent; they deny the characteristic of mere conceptualization, the characteristic of dependence, and the real characteristic of all things."[44]

Having dismissed both extremes of being and nonbeing, the Siddha Lui then asks, "Who believes in such an enlightenment?" This question directs the attention to the mind that conceives of "being" and "nonbeing." This mind, which can become fixated on the notions of being or nonbeing, can by the same token detach itself from these views to attain the subtle poise of the center, the Middle Way.

The Way, Lui says, is inscrutable to conception; Sporting in the triple world, I cannot be detected.

The *Sandhinirmocana sutra* says, "Someone in ignorance who clings to the signs of the world because of overwhelming interest in perceptual and cognitive signs thus cannot think of, or assess, or believe in, the ultimate nirvana that obliterates all signs so that reification ends."[45] The early Zen master Tao- hsin wrote, "Those who cultivate the Way and attain real emptiness do not see emptiness or nonemptiness; they have no views."

The "triple world" ordinarily refers to the totality of conditioned existence, specifically the realms of desire, form, and formless abstraction. Munidatta here takes the term to mean body, speech, and mind. Either way—and there is no real contradiction between these two interpretations—"sporting in the triple world" refers to freedom of action. The liberated one "cannot be detected" in the sense that there is no fixation on any object, and no identification with things. As a Zen proverb describes this freedom, "The gods offering flowers find no road to strew them on, demons and outsiders secretly spying cannot see."

He to whom color, character,
and figure are not known—
How can he discourse on scriptural knowledge?

This couplet follows on the preceding to counter the drift toward denial. as repudiated in the quotation from scripture cited in the comments on the first couplet. Realization of emptiness does not mean destruction or disappearance of characteristics. In Zen terms, misconstrued emptiness results in a kind of ignorance in which one "calls a pitcher a bell," or "points to a deer and says it's a horse."

You will present me with questions,
"Whose?""What?"
Like the moon in the water, it is neither real nor false.

"Whose" questions the subject in relation to the object, "what" questions the object in relation to the subject. The "moon in the water" is a reflection, representing the relation, or relativity, of the reflecting subject and reflected object; "neither real nor false" means neither absolutely existent nor absolutely nonexistent. Here again the mind of the practitioner is directed toward the Middle Way by detachment from one-sided views.

Lui says, "As long as I will be,
The one with whom I am will be unseen."

In Buddhist terms, the sense of identification with acquired habits of thought and attitude is a false self. The real self is the Buddha-nature, which is "permanent, pure, blissful self." As long as the false self is the center of subjective operation, the true self remains obscure.

The uncovering of the true self is also directly connected to the uncovering of the true nature of phenomena. The Japanese Zen master Dogen wrote, "Studying Buddhism is studying the self; studying the self is forgetting the self. Forgetting the self is being enlightened by all things." As long as subjective attitudes and ideas reign, the objective nature of things is obscured.

Viewed in another way, this final couplet sums up by illustrating the identity and distinction of existence and emptiness. In terms of essence, subject and object are both empty of absoluteness, yet in terms of characteristics, subject and object are not without apparent factuality. "As long as I will be, the one with whom I am" alludes to essential identity on the level of absolute truth, while being "unseen" refers to experiential distinction on the level of relative truth.

27

BHUSUKU

The clouds of compassion pervade endlessly,
Smashing the duality of being and nonbeing.
Up in the middle of the sky, wondrous;
Behold, Bhusuku, the natural essence.
When quiet, one's own mind gives a cry of cheer,
On hearing which the web of the senses is rent.
In ecstasy have I realized purity of objects,
Like the moon shining in the sky.
In this triplex world, this much indeed's essential;
Bhusuku the Yogi opens up the darkness.

The clouds of compassion pervade endlessly,
Smashing the duality of being and nonbeing.

Compassion, in the Buddhist sense, is not just emotional feeling; it is at once the orientation and energy of living Buddhist philosophy. The common weal for which the Buddhist strives is twofold, mundane and transmundane. Mundane weal refers to the peace and happiness of the world, while transmundane weal refers to liberation from slavery to ego and things.

If apparent reality were a fixed absolute, there would be no possibility of freedom or change, and therefore no inspiration, no leeway, and no use for Buddhistic compassion. If apparent reality had no psychological reality, on the other hand, everyone would already be liberated and would have no needs; so there would be no reason, no need, and no scope for Buddhistic compassion.

By realizing the emptiness of absoluteness in conditioned states, the Buddhist is enabled to be compassionate without the limitation of strictly personal emotion. By realizing the relative and psychological realities of conditioned states, the Buddhist is motivated to extend compassion without the limitation of personal aloofness. Thus the nonduality of being and nonbeing is realized in the experience and exercise of objective compassion.

Up in the middle of the sky, wondrous;
Behold, Bhusuku, the natural essence.

The middle of the sky represents emptiness, specifically in terms of its identity to the Middle Way beyond the duality of being and nonbeing, the essential nature of all things.

It is in this sense that the *Flower Ornament Scripture* says, "Sentient beings and phenomena are null and void in essence, like space, with no location. Attaining this spacelike knowledge, one is forever free from grasping and clinging; like space, it has no variation and is unobstructed in the world."

Speaking of the inner clarification that prepares the mind to perceive the essential nature of things, the same scripture also says, "If you want to know the realm of Buddhahood, make your mind as clear as space; detach from subjective imaginings and from all grasping, making your mind unimpeded wherever it turns." It is important to realize, from a practical point of view, that this is not the same experience as the exercise of absorption in space, or *gaganatalasamadhi,* which is sometimes practiced by Buddhists as part of a method of loosening subjective attachment to conditioned perceptual and conceptual biases.

This pragmatic distinction is made clear by the 13th-century Zen master Dogen, who wrote, "Those who claim to have fulfilled Zen study and assume the rank of teacher, while they hear the voice of the nature of things and see the forms of the nature of things, yet their bodies and minds, their experiences of object and subject, just continue to rise and fall in the pit of confusion. What this is like is *wrongly thinking that the nature of things will appear when the whole world we perceive is obliterated, that the nature of things is not the present totality of phenomena.*"[46]

When quiet, one's own mind gives a cry of cheer,
On hearing which the web of the senses is rent.

Quieting the habitually ruminating mind allows room for intuitive understanding to surface into consciousness in a functional manner. This breaks routine fixation on the surface appearances of externals.

The 11th-century Zen master Yuan-wu wrote, "Just still the thoughts in your mind. It is good to do this right in the midst of disturbance." This makes it clear that this quietude is an inner method of releasing potential, not a habit of eremitic quietism. Neither does it refer to a temporary forced stilling of thought trains, but something more profound, as Yuan-wu also explained in his writings: "Let go of all your previous imaginings, opinions, interpretations, worldly knowledge, intellectualism, egoism, and competitiveness. Become like a dead tree, like cold ashes. When you reach the point where feelings are ended, views are gone, and your mind is clean and naked, you open up to realization."

In ecstasy have I realized purity of objects,
Like the moon shining in the sky.

In ecstasy, beyond conceptual thought, the eye of direct perception sees things as they are without subjective projections or interpretations. Purity, in Buddhist metaphysics, means emptiness of inherent identity. Here, the moon shining in the sky represents awareness of essential emptiness. The *Flower Ornament Scripture* says, "In each moment of mind are infinite lands produced; by the spiritual power of the enlightened, all are seen as pure."

In this triplex world, this much indeed's essential; Bhusuku the Yogi opens up the darkness.

It is realizing the essential emptiness of what we consider the world itself, whether in the realm of desire, the realm of form, or the realm of formless abstraction, that ultimately disperses the impermeable darkness of naive material realism. In the *Dhammapada,* Buddha says, "It is better to live one day seeing the ultimate truth than to live a hundred years without seeing the ultimate truth."[47]

28

ARYADEVA

Where the wind of the senses
has vanished from the mind,
I don't know where my self has gone.
Wonderful—the drum of compassion is sounding!
Aryadeva reigns without support.
It appears like the light of the moon;
The mind, transforming, enters unresisting therein.
Giving up worldly habits of fear and hate,
Seeking, seeking, scrutinize emptiness.
Aryadeva has destroyed everything;
He wards off fear and hate from afar.

Where the wind of the senses
has vanished from the mind,
I don't know where my self has gone.

The visceral or instinctive sense of selfhood, revolving around desire and fear, attraction and aversion, in pursuit of self-gratification and self-preservation, is intimately connected to, or one might say a quality of, the relationship of the organism to the sensory environment. The sociopsychological sense of selfhood also involves desire and fear, attraction and aversion, self-gratification and self-preservation, but with greater complexity of subject matter, including much that is of a more subtle nature than the subject matter of instinctive or visceral self-consciousness.

In contemporary terms, for example, self-esteem is spoken of almost as if it were a material substance; and indeed it can actually involve material substances in the overall composition of its subject matter. Whether one considers the abstract psychological patterns or the actual content of attention in the concrete operation of these patterns, the relationship between the core of consciousness and the data of the senses is crucial to the nature and quality of the experience of the empirical self.

In Buddhist thought, this much is considered to be well-established fact. But in terms of Buddhist philosophy and psychology, which are not two separate fields, representations of facts of this nature are not made for acceptance as dogma, but for practical structure in meditation. So it is not a philosophical problem, but a meditative task, involving a very specific kind of introspection, that the Siddha presents in the second line of the couplet: When the subject matter of self-consciousness is discounted, where is the self?

Wonderful—the drum of compassion is sounding!
Aryadeva reigns without support.

In one of the most famous of Zen stories, a seeker asked the founder of Zen, "Please enable me to attain peace of mind." The Zen founder responded, "Bring me your mind, and I will set it at peace." The seeker said, "When I search for my mind,

I cannot grasp it." The Zen founder said, "I have set your mind at peace."

When one carries out the meditation described in the first couplet, the attention bypasses all objects, sensory or abstract, ultimately to find nothing graspable. This ungraspability is one classical definition of emptiness, and this particular exercise is a well known method of inducing the experience of emptiness. When the climax or consummation is reached, when ungraspability is no longer just a concept but a direct experience, instead of falling into an abyss the mind opens up into an inconceivable realm, which the ancients used to call *thusness.*

Thusness is the actual substance of objective compassion, what Buddhists and neo-Taoists sometimes call the "wondrous existence" that is identical to "true emptiness." It is at once inconceivable and undeniable; for this reason, allusions to the experience may often appear paradoxical from an ordinary point of view.

To merge with thusness, according to an eminent Zen master of ancient times, one must realize that "you are not it; it is you." An earlier Zen master said, "A sage has no self, but there is nothing that is not the self." This is the stage of "forgetting the self to be enlightened by all things," and the time when artificiality is dropped to merge consciously with the natural.

Not dwelling on anything external or internal, the mind is "without support." That means it is not leaning on anything. Centered and aware, this undistracted mind "reigns" over its faculties as an autonomous overseer.

It appears like the light of the moon;
The mind, transforming, enters unresisting therein.

This couplet represents the mind being liberated from the limitations imposed by absorption in matter, form, and habits of thought. In terminology commonly associated with Zen, Munidatta describes the experience illustrated here as the Mind-King attaining mindlessness and merging with pure radiance, as discriminatory thought loses its influence. With the mind absorbed in naturalness, he continues, the darkness of discriminatory thinking is dissolved; this is "entering unresisting into the light."

Giving up worldly habits of fear and hate,
Seeking, seeking, scrutinize emptiness.

The *Flower Ornament Scripture* says, "What happens to all fears with the attainment of the stage of joy, fears such as fear of not surviving, fear of ill repute, fear of death, fear of states of misery, fear of intimidation by groups, is that all such fears leave. Why is that? Inasmuch as the very concept of self is gone, there is no self-love, much less any love for material things."[48] When there is no fear, there is no aversion; the defensiveness of the ego is gone.

This state of mind is not a product of ordinary sentiments like boldness or indifference, nor is it an outcome of the abnegation of a self secretly treasured as real. Rather, it is a result of the realization of emptiness, experientially impressed upon the psyche as a result of first-hand search and discovery. Here the Siddha uses the word *biara,* "examine, scrutinize," from Sanskrit *vicara* (an intellectual function active in the first stage of meditation), further describing it as deliberate and purposeful, underscoring the fact that realization of "emptiness" comes about through penetrating insight, and has nothing to do with ignoring reality.

Aryadeva has destroyed everything;
He wards off fear and hate from afar.

Destroying everything is a familiar representation of realizing the emptiness, the voidness of inherent selfhood, in all things. This "wards off fear and hate from afar" in that the transcendence experienced through emptiness is not suppression of states of mind that have already arisen, but rather dissolution of the very basis of compulsive reaction to conditions. This pragmatic distinction is made clear in the saying of Bunan, a Japanese Zen master of the 17th century, that "It is easy to be detached from things; it is harder to be inaccessible to things."

29

SARAHA

No dot, no crescent; no sun, no moon—
The Mind King is free of everything.
Going straight ahead, straight ahead,
don't take a turn on the road!
Enlightenment is near at hand;
don't go to a distant land!
The protective band is on your wrist;
don't get a mirror.
Self is realized by oneself, in one's own mind.
Roaring on the Other Shore,
In the midst of bad people he goes on aloof.
Of the canals and watercourses to the left and right,
Saraha says, "My dear, the straight way appeals!"

No dot, no crescent; no sun, no moon—
The Mind King is free of everything.

The dot and crescent, orthographical marks indicating nasalization and thus associated with the sacred syllables *Om* and *Hum,* symbolically represent the sun and moon, which in turn represent formless and formal cognition, absolute and relative thought of enlightenment. Here the Siddha refers directly to the absolute itself, beyond all possibility of representation and expression.

The extraordinary Sung dynasty Zen master Fo-yen said, "Only when you have arrived at the state where there is no delusion and no enlightenment are you comfortable and saving energy to a maximum degree."[49] This is the aim to which the Bengali adept Saraha refers in this introductory couplet. This allusion is not made simply as a statement of an ideal or a goal, but more immediately as an indication of orientation.

Going straight ahead, straight ahead,
don't take a turn on the road!
Enlightenment is near at hand;
don't go to a distant land!

One of the apparent paradoxes commonplace to universalist Buddhism is the principle that enlightenment is not an attainment. In terms of objective reality, this means that truth is so of itself and is not an intellectual construction. In terms of subjective reality, this means that the capacities of the enlightened mind are not acquired but uncovered, not produced but developed. The ultimate directness, in these terms, the straight path *par excellence,* is actual pragmatic realization, disinterment, so to speak, of what has always been there. As Fo-yen said, "Buddhism is a most economical affair, conserving the most energy; it has always been present, but you do not understand."[50] Realizing this in life experience is the straight way.

The protective band is on your wrist;
don't get a mirror.
Self is realized by oneself, in one's own mind.

This couplet underscores the teaching that enlightenment is not obtained from outside. In the *Dhammapada,* Buddha is reported to have said, "I have overcome all, I know all, I am unaffected by all things. Leaving everything behind, having ended craving, I am freed. Having understood on my own, to whom should I attribute it?"[51] The famous Sung dynasty Zen master Ta Hui wrote, "Buddha means awake, being aware everywhere and always. Seeing Buddha everywhere means seeing your own inherent natural Buddha in the fundamental wellspring of your self."[52]

Roaring on the Other Shore,
In the midst of bad people he goes on aloof.

The Other Shore is transcendence; roaring means that this is not quietism. In Zen terms, those who have attained true transcendence and liberation are able to "enter into the realms of both Buddhas and devils," whereas quietists are "only able to enter the realm of Buddhas, not the realm of devils." In other words, the contrived detachment of the quietist is dependent upon an artifically controlled environment, whereas the authentic transcendence of the self-realized is independent of the surroundings. It is axiomatic in Buddhism, furthermore, that the enlightened enter in among the unenlightened to fulfill the purpose of enlightenment.

Of the canals and watercourses to the left and right, Saraha says, "My dear, the straight way appeals!"

The canals and watercourses to the left and right refer to the network of psychic energy channels and focal points utilized in contemplative visualization exercises. The straight way, metaphysically speaking, is the Middle Way, beyond being and nothingness; psychophysically speaking, it is the central channel of purification, beyond perception and dalliance. Here the Siddha insists on the central realization, warning the seeker not to cling to either being or nothingness, either materialism or quietism; and not to wander "tripping" in psychic states, bemused by perception and dalliance.

30

DHENDHANA

My house has no neighbor on settled land.
There is no rice in the pot—I am ever the guest.
Samsara goes on whirling around;
How can milk, after milking, go back into the teat?
The bull gave birth; the cow is sterile.
The jar's being milked, all day and night.
The intelligent one is ignorant,
The thief is a policeman.
Day after day, the jackal fights with the lion;
Few understand the song of Dhendhana's verse.

My house has no neighbor on settled land.
There is no rice in the pot—I am ever the guest.

Realizing that the secondary "self" resulting from social and psychological conditioning is not an absolute reality, one ceases to identify oneself in terms of the surroundings. This is "having no neighbors," or, in Zen terms, "not keeping company with myriad things."

Realizing that things of the world are impermanent, one ceases to think of personal possessions as appurtenances of the self. This is having "no rice in the pot." Being nevertheless in the temporal world, all the while realizing the transitoriness of the empirical self as well as of all things, one is in the world without being of the world; this is being "ever the guest."

Samsara goes on whirling around;
How can milk, after milking, go back into the teat?

Samsara is the flux of conditioned states, in which what goes before influences what comes along afterward. On one level, samsara means the flow of thoughts in self-conditioning patterns of habit. If the mind goes along with the flow, it will not be possible to return to the source.

The bull gave birth; the cow is sterile.
The jar's being milked, all day and night.

One method of meditation on emptiness considers the relativity of cause and effect. If a cause is only a cause relative to its effect, then the effect must coexist with the cause; but if the effect is already there, the cause cannot be the cause of that effect, and the effect cannot be the effect of that cause. Similarly, considering that nothing temporal exists of itself but depends on conditions, how can those conditions themselves exist in order to produce something?

It is important to understand that these meditations are not philosophy as understood in the conventional Western sense. Nor are they mysterious oriental paradoxes to be entertained intellectually. Meditations of this kind are designed to enable the mind to register the limitations of linear t hinking.

The apparent paradox of an "effect without a cause" is called "inconceivable existence," here symbolically represented as a "bull giving birth." The apparent paradox of a "cause without an effect" is called "true emptiness," here symbolically represented as a "sterile cow."

Such imagery is common in Zen tradition, wherein it is not used for bafflement or destruction of reason (as touted by certain popularizers of irrationalism who confuse mystification with mysticism) but for encapsulating directions for those meditation practices that lead to direct experience of the inadequacy of linear thinking. This makes it possible to transcend the limitations of conditioned thought without abnormally suppressing or warping the intellect.

According to Munidatta, "milking the jar," taking something out of the vessel rather than putting something in, represents actual realization of essencelessness, or emptiness of intrinsic nature. In the *Sandhinirmocana-sutra,* Buddha explains, "When I say all things have no essence, I am alluding to three kinds of essencelessness: essencelessness of characteristics, essencelessness of birth, and ultimate essencelessness.

"What is the essencelessness of characteristics of all things? It is their conceptually grasped character. Why? Because the characteristics are defined by artificial names, not by inherent definition. Therefore this is called the essencelessness of characteristics.

"What is the essencelessness of birth of things? It is the dependently originated character of things. Why? Because they exist dependent on the power of other conditions and do not exist of themselves. Therefore this is called the essencelessness of birth.

"What is the ultimate essencelessness of things? It means that things are said to be essenceless because of the essencelessness of birth; that is to say the fact of dependent origination is also called ultimate essencelessness. Why? I reveal the pure object of attention in things to be ultimate essencelessness. Dependency is not a pure object of attention, so I also call it ultimately essenceless."[53]

The intelligent one is ignorant,
The thief is a policeman.

Conventional intelligence, insofar as it is dealing with the conceptually grasped characteristics of things, is therefore ignorant of the absolute nature of things. Insofar as the conventional intellect grasps things and appropriates them into its preconditioned worldview, it is a thief. On the other hand, when intelligence is used to analyze things to understand their conditionality, recognize their transitoriness, and arrive at the emptiness of inherent nature, inspiring the thought of enlightenment, it thus prevents appearances from occasioning delusion; so the "thief" turns out to be a "policeman."

Day after day, the jackal fights with the lion;
Few understand the song of Dhendhana's verse.

The jackal is clinging, compulsive, conditioned thinking and conceptualization; the lion is realization of emptiness, insight into absolute truth. The meaning of the jackal fighting with the lion is explained in the *Sandhinirmocana-sutra* in these terms: "People produce explanations of the dependent and real natures based on the characteristics of the conceptualized nature, saying they are such and such, in accord with how people conceptualize them. Because the explanations condition their minds, because their awareness conforms to the explanations, because they are lulled by the explanation, they cling to their conceptualizations of the dependent nature and the real nature as such and so.

"Because they cling to their conceptualizations of the dependent and real natures, this condition produces the dependent nature of the future, and due to this condition people may be defiled by afflictions, actions, or birth, and forever rush around in repetitious cycles, with no rest, suffering pains and vexations, going through all kinds of psychological states."[54]

The jackal fights with the lion because it feels threatened with annihilation. This is why "few people understand," as the Siddha says. As a Zen proverb has it, "The roar of the lion bursts the brains of the jackal."

31

DARIKA

By the practice of nonseparateness
of emptiness and compassion,
physically, verbally, and mentally,
Darika sports on the Other Shore of the sky.
What are mantras to you? What are Tantras to you?
What are meditation and elucidation to you?
In the effortless play of nondependence
is indescribably ultimate nirvana.
Considering sorrow and happiness one,
the knower enjoys the senses:
Mind above everything,
Darika feels neither self nor nonself.
O King, O King, O King! The other kings are bound!
By the kindness of Lui's lotus feet,
Darika's attained the twelfth stage.

**By the practice of nonseparateness
of emptiness and compassion,
physically, verbally, and mentally,
Darika sports on the Other Shore of the sky.**

Body, speech, and mind, or thought, word, and deed, are referred to in Tantric Buddhism as the Three Mysteries; in essence of the same nature as the universe itself, the three mysteries are the medium through which the individual identifies with the cosmic Buddha.

The "other shore of the sky" is the state of the practitioner gone beyond realization of emptiness *qua* emptiness. The *Flower Ornament Scripture* describes this as being "empty, signless, wishless, yet with compassion and kindness," and being "in the world with great forbearance, having acquired detachment; having extinguished the flames of afflictions and stilled worldly cravings, coursing in the nonduality of things as like reflections, illusions, dreams, yet showing compassion."

In terms of the structure of meditation, this is illustrated in the T'ien-t'ai "stopping and seeing" practice, wherein one first contemplates the conditional nature of things in order to enter into contemplation of their ultimate emptiness, then contemplates the conditional nature of things in order to re-emerge from emptiness into relativity. Going back and forth between contemplation of these two facets of conditionality, finally one attains the central balance of the Middle Way.

The classical Zen master Pai-chang said, "A Buddha is just someone outside of bondage who comes back inside of bondage to be a Buddha in this way; someone beyond birth and death, someone on the other side of mystic annihilation, who comes back to this side to act thus as a Buddha." He also said, "A Buddha does not remain in Buddhahood; this is called the real field of blessings." Such is the "nonseparateness of emptiness and compassion" to which the Siddha refers in this couplet.

The inscrutable mind is in great ecstasy;
Darika sports on the Other Shore of the sky.

The inscrutable mind is gone beyond both form and emptiness. Pai-chang said, "Just don't be obstructed by being or nothingness, and do not abide in nonobstruction, and have no knowledge or understandng of nonabiding. This is called spiritual power. When you do not even cling to this spiritual power, it is called having no spiritual power, so you are like the saying, 'Footsteps of a bodhisattva with no spiritual power cannot be found.' This is someone beyond Buddha, most inconceivable."

What are mantras to you? What are Tantras to you?
What are meditation and elucidation to you?
In the effortless play of nondependence
is indescribably ultimate nirvana.

This couplet speaks of transcending the means when the end is attained, but the first line also provokes the question of one's relation to the teaching to begin with. For those who approach it with ambition, greed, or other impure egotistic motives, the teaching is said to be "golden chains." The T'ang dynasty Zen master Lin-chi also said, "Although gold dust is precious, when it gets in your eyes it blinds you."

Zen master Yen-t'ou, a contemporary of Lin-chi, explained this point quite clearly:" The moment you prize anything, it has turned into a nest, a dodge. The ancients called this clothing sticking to the body, an ailment most difficult to cure. When I was traveling in the past, I called on teachers in one or two places; they just taught day and night concentration, sitting until your buttocks grow callouses, yet all the while your mouth is drooling. From the start they sit in the utter darkness in the belly of the primordial Buddha and ignorantly say they are sitting in meditation, conserving this attainment. At such times, there is still desire there!

"Have you not heard the saying, 'When independent and unimpassioned, you yourself are Buddha'? An ancient remarked, 'If you poison the milk, even clarified butter is deadly.'

"This is not something you attain by hearing, not something you reach or abide in, not something in your forms! Don't misperceive what is merely a gate or a door."[55]

Considering sorrow and happiness one,
the knower enjoys the senses:
Mind above everything,
Darika feels neither self nor nonself.

The early Zen master Seng-ts'an, considered the Third Patriarch of Chinese Zen, wrote, "The Great Way is without difficulty; just avoid discriminating." He also wrote, "If you want to gain the way of oneness, don't be averse to the six sense fields. The six sense fields are not bad; after all they're the same as true awakening." The enjoyment of the senses that is not limited by aversion to pain or sorrow and attraction to pleasure or happiness is the experience of enlightened knowledge and perception. Neither identifying nor rejecting, the mind is beyond the world even in the midst of the world.

O King, O King, O King! The other kings are bound!
By the kindness of Lui's lotus feet,
Darika's attained the twelfth stage.

When the "central government" of the mind is independent and autonomous, it cannot be overwhelmed by temporary states; it can employ its faculties without being confused or deluded by their operations.

The kindness of lotus feet refers to compassionate, enlightened guidance. Lui, many of whose own Tantric songs appear in this collection, was evidently Darika's teacher. The twelfth stage is the supreme realization of Buddhism. The highest stage of bodhisattvahood is the tenth, which is called "Cloud of Teaching." Above this, the eleventh stage, is basic buddhahood, called "Equal Enlightenment." Beyond this is the twelfth stage, the final goal, called "Sublime Enlightenment."

32

BHADE

So long have I been self-deluded;
Now I've understood, enlightened by a true teacher.
Now the Mind King is my lord;
It rolls into the sea of the sky.
I see the ten directions all empty;
Outside mind there is neither sin nor virtue.
Told by a Vajrayana master
the hiding place of liberation,
I have supped on the water of the sky.
Bhade says, "Misfortune has come!
I have devoured the Mind King!"

So long have I been self-deluded;
Now I've understood, enlightened by a true teacher.

Self-delusion, keeping the mind in confinement within subjective opinion, bias, and sentiment, is the factor that makes an outside source of guidance necessary. Without a source of objective insight, subjectivity processes everything in terms of its existing predilections and prejudices.

Even when there is a true teacher at hand, subjective biases based on truthless elements like wishful thinking can distort or obstruct reception of truthful input. For this reason it is also necessary for the seeker to reach forward from a deeper level than the psychological self. Part of reaching forward in this way is seeking truth by inner reality, without preconceptions of what outward form it may take.

Now the Mind King is my lord;
It rolls into the sea of the sky.

Enlightenment by a true teacher, understanding that the acquired self is not the real Buddha-nature, one is able to distinguish the temporal from the primal and become conscious of the essence of mind. When attention is successfully focused on this essence, it is not confined by the realms of desires, forms, and abstractions. The sea of the sky stands for the realization of emptiness that ensues, as well as the feeling that this experiential realization engenders. The experience, which is like a total perception, is not a blackout or a blank, but it does feel like slipping into a boundless openness. This can be thrilling at first, but when the experience is properly digested, it leads to spontaneous natural ecstasy.

I see the ten directions all empty;
Outside mind there is neither sin nor virtue.

One of the major awakenings of the Japanese Pure Land saint Ippen took place as he watched children at play, spinning tops. Watching them spin for a time and then fall still, Ippen reflected that the good and evil of the world is like a top; spin it and it turns, don't spin it and it stops.

In his *Ten Mysterious Gates,* the great Flower Ornament Buddhist master Chih-yen wrote. "Good and bad are according to the operation of mind, so it is called creation by operation of the mind. Since there is no separate realm of objects outside of mind, we say 'only mind.' If it operates harmoniously, it is called nirvana; that is why the scripture says, 'Mind makes the Buddhas.' If it operates perversely, it is samsara; that is why the scripture says, 'The triple world is illusory; it is only made by the mind.'"[56]

The *Dhammapada* begins with Buddha's sayings, "Everything has mind in the lead, has mind in the forefront, is made by mind. If one speaks or acts with a corrupt mind, misery will follow as the wheel of the cart follows the foot of the ox.

"Everything has mind in the lead, has mind in the forefront, is made by mind. If one speaks or acts with a pure mind, happiness will follow like a shadow that never leaves."[57]

Told by a Vajrayana master
the hiding place of liberation,
I have supped on the water of the sky.

An ancient Zen master said, "Let your hiding place have no traces, but do not hide in tracelessness." The hiding place that has no traces is the innermost essence of mind not fixed on objects; this is "the hiding place of liberation." The tracelessness in which one should not hide is attachment to detachment, or in extreme cases oblivion; as a Zen proverb says, "Stagnant water cannot contain the coils of a dragon. "Therefore the Siddha says he has supped on the water of the sky, the fluid living energy of emptiness, freedom, release.

Bhade says, "Misfortune has come!
I have devoured the Mind King!"

Abiding in the state of the Mind King results in what is called "mirroring awareness." While this is a fundamental initiatory experience, and subsequently a basic tool, of Zen and Mahamudra practice, the same provisions apply to this as to all expedient teachings of Buddhism.

Classical Zen master Pai-chang said, "To speak of the mirror awareness is still not really right; by way of the impure, discern the pure. If you say the immediate mirrorlike awareness is correct, or that there is something else beyond mirroring awareness, both are delusion. If you keep dwelling in the immediate mirrorlike awareness, this too is delusion, referred to as the error of naturalism."

With typical Vajrayana skill, Bhade expresses all of these meanings. A Zen proverb says, "Ascending from earth to sky is easy; coming down to earth from the sky is hard."

33

KRISHNACARYA

The arm of emptiness, striking with suchness,
Has brought everything back to the capital of illusion.
He slumbers unaware of difference
between self and other;
Krishna the naked mendicant
has gone to sleep in naturalness.
Without consciousness or sense, he's in a deep sleep;
Having done everything successfully,
he's aslumber in felicity.
In a dream I have seen
the emptiness of triplex existence,
Turning back beyond coming and going.
The master Jalandhari will be a witness;
The top scholars notice no bias in me.

The arm of emptiness, striking with suchness,
Has brought everything back to the capital of illusion.

The *Sandhinirmocana-sutra* says, "Inasmuch as the conceptualized characteristics in transient appearances, on which are based the conceptualizations that are the sphere of discrimination, are not actually true, therefore this inherent essencelessness, true thusness in which phenomena have no identity, the pure focus of attention, is called ultimate reality." [58]

Illusion is seen to be illusion on emptying the mind and seeing thusness without preconceptions. The *Sandinirmocanasutra* also says, "The characteristic of conceptual grasping can be known through the association of names and characterizations. The characteristic of dependent origination can be known through the conceptual clinging superimposed on dependent existence. The perfect characteristic of reality can be known by not clinging to conceptions superimposed on dependent existence."[59]

He slumbers unaware of difference
between self and other;
Krishna the naked mendicant
has gone to sleep in naturalness.

Slumber, sleep, and unawareness represent a state of mind unencumbered by preoccupation with superficial appearances. Nakedness symbolizes purity of mind, mendicancy symbolizes nonattachment, or purity of heart, being in the world but not of it. The Yuan dynasty Zen master Yuansou said, "The mind of people of the Way is straight as a bowstring. Simply because they are not burdened by ideas of others and self, of right and wrong, of sacred and profane, of better and worse, or by deception, falsehood, flattery, or deviousness, they spontaneously gain access to the substance of mind that dwells on nothing."[60]

Without consciousness or sense, he's in a deep sleep;
Having done everything successfully,
he's aslumber in felicity.

Before Buddha was enlightened, he learned to attain a state of abstract trance referred to as "neither perception nor non-perception." This was supposedly considered, in his day, the most exalted state one could attain. Buddha went beyond this to a state called "cessation of all perception and sensation," but he realized that this is still not really nirvana, not spiritual liberation.

The *Sandhinirmocana-sutra* says, "Even if enlightening beings are versed in the mysteries of mind, intellect, and consciousness based on knowledge of reality, nevertheless the Buddha does not consider them to be versed in all the mysteries of mind, intellect, and consciousness. If enlightening beings inwardly truly do not see clinging or clinging consciousness, do not see repository or repository consciousness, do not see accumulation, do not see mind, do not see the eye, form, or eye-consciousness, do not see ear, sound, or ear-consciousness, do not see nose, scent, or nose-consciousness, do not see tongue, flavor, or tongue-consciousness, do not see body, feeling, or bodyconsciousness, do not see intellect, phenomena, or conceptual consciousness, then they are called enlightening beings well versed in ultimate truth."[61]

Having no consciousness or sense, in the context of universalist and Tantric Buddhism, is not meant literally, but alludes to realization of ultimate truth, generally referred to as emptiness and thus commonly depicted or approached by negations. In terms of personal experience, this couplet speaks of consciousness experienced as "radiant" rather than bent on itself, sensing all things as if "lighting" the universe, rather than leaping around, or mucking about, from one object, or one narrow focus, to another.

In a dream I have seen
the emptiness of triplex existence,
Turning back beyond coming and going.

The first line of this couplet describes perception of emptiness in the relativity of subject and object. Dreaming is not only a symbol of this particular aspect of relativity; in Buddhist Yoga, the phenomenon of dreaming is also considered a demonstration or proof of relativity and the emptiness of phenomena as conceptually grasped.

In the second line, "turning back" refers to the mental revolution whereby one ceases to view subjectively projected conceptualizations as objectively intrinsic characteristics of things. This enables one to place the attention on a level of reality that is "beyond coming and going" in the sense that consciousness is not fixated on transient appearances.

The master Jalandhari will be a witness;
The top scholars notice no bias in me.

Jalandhari, a Siddha or adept, seems to have been the teacher of Krishnacarya; the reference here is not, however, to formal authority, but to objective knowledge. Emptiness, in the Buddhist sense, has been defined by one Hindu scholar as freedom from prejudice. When one actually witnesses emptiness experientially, then cultural and intellectual biases cannot be maintained; there is then no conflict or contradiction, furthermore, between intellectual understanding and intuitive insight. Able to deal effectively with the ordinary world while at the same time spiritually and psychologically liberated by realization of emptiness, one attains the supreme balance of the Middle Way.

34

TARAKA

I have no self: how can there be attachment?
In the Great Symbol, desire is broken down.
Realize naturalness; don't forget, O Yogi!
You'll be completely released, be however you are.
So far so good;
On the road of naturalness, Yogi,
don't remain in confusion.
Castration and hernia are known when swimming;
How can what is beyond
the range of words be explained?
Taraka says there's no chance here—
Whoever understands, there's a rope around his neck.

I have no self: how can there be attachment?
In the Great Symbol, desire is broken down.

The Great Symbol, Mahamudra in Sanskrit, is the Tantric equivalent to Zen Buddhism. They are no different in essence, though techniques may vary within both traditions. Based on the immaculate mind, the essential great symbol practice is like the exercise of the "mirroring awareness" often referred to by the classical Zen master Pai-chang, who lived in the eighth and ninth centuries. This is when Old School Tibetan Buddhism, the Nyingma, including Mahamudra practice, was established in Tibet.

In practical terms, "having no self" means not being imprisoned in subjectivity. This is the experience, commonly referred to in Buddhist literature, of shedding the duality of subject and object in direct perception. The 17th-century Zen master Bunan wrote, "Just see directly and hear directly. When seeing directly, there is no seer; when hearing directly, there is no hearer." He also wrote, "One who sees, hears, feels, and knows without subjectivity is called a living Buddha." That is what this means.

The 13th-century Zen master Dogen expressed this practical process brilliantly in his famous essay *The Issue at Hand,* wherein he wrote, "To act upon and witness myriad things with the burden of the self is delusion; to act upon and witness the self in the advent of myriad things is enlightenment." He also wrote, "The study of Buddhism is study of the self. To learn about the self is to forget the self. To forget the self is to be enlightened by all things."[62]

The Mahamudra or Great Symbol experience is also called the *Sagara-mudra-samadhi,* or absorption symbolized by the ocean. This refers to an oceanic, all-at-once consciousness of the totality of everything. This state of mind shatters attachment to subjective discrimination, so attention is not fixated on particular objects. Thus it is that "desire is broken down," because there is an overwhelming sense of unity and fullness of experience, leaving no room for wishful thinking at all.

Realize naturalness; don't forget, O Yogi!
You'll be completely released, be however you are.

Zen master Bunan said, "To acquiesce to the teaching of enlightenment as it is, directly abandon all things, merge with the body of thusness, and experience peerless peace and bliss, is no more than a matter of whether or not you think of yourself." He also wrote, "Become dead while alive, completely, then whatever you do, as you will, is good ."

So far so good;
On the road of naturalness, Yogi,
don't remain in confusion.

The 13th-century Zen master Lan-hsi, one of the first in Japan, wrote of the difference between natural enlightenment and artificial confusion in a seminal treatise on Zen meditation: "Your own light of wisdom is clear and bright of itself, but when obscured by false ideas you lose this and therefore create illusions." Sho-itsu, another 13th-century Zen master instrumental in the establishment of this teaching in Japan, expressed naturalness in this way: "Zen is not conception or perception; if you establish an idea, you turn away from the source. The Way is beyond cultivated effects; if you set up accomplishment, you lose the essence."

Castration and hernia are known when swimming;
How can what is beyond
the range of words be explained?

Trying to pursue spiritual practices through the agency of egocentered artificiality does not eliminate moral and psychological weaknesses and defects; it actually makes them even more evident, sometimes more dramatic and more exaggerated, than in the context of the hypocrisy of ordinary life.

One aspect of such a problematic approach to spiritual studies is the attempt to reduce the transcendental to cliches, or to encompass the inconceivable within preconceptions. This manner of study is not only spiritually impotent and sterile; because of the conceit it engenders, it causes egoism to protrude even more grotesquely than it does on the level of mundane social, emotional, and intellectual life.

This is why the state of realization to which these Tantric Siddhas are pointing is called naturalness.

Taraka says there's no chance here—
Whoever understands, there's a rope around his neck.

An ancient Japanese Buddhist poem says, "There is no way in all the world; even in the remote mountains, the deer cries in autumn." The Zen classic known as *The Blue Cliff Record* says, "Even if you can grasp it before it is spoken of, still this is remaining in the shell, wandering in limitation; even if you penetrate at a single phrase, you still won't avoid insane views on the way." The same work also says, "One who can take action on the road is like a tiger in the mountains; one immersed in worldly understanding is like a monkey in a cage."[63]

35

SARAHA

The body is a boat, mind is the rudder;
Hold the helm, guiding the vessel,
by the instruction of a true teacher.
Hold the rudder with a steady mind—
There's no other way to the other shore.
A boatman pulls a boat by a rope;
Give it up and go by naturalness alone.
There's terror on the road; brigands are strong.
All is told in the fluctuation of the world.
To the shore, he goes upstream in the swift current:
Saraha says, "It is proved in the sky."

The body is a boat, mind is the rudder;
Hold the helm, guiding the vessel,
by the instruction of a true teacher.

According to the *Dhammapada,* Buddha said, "The mind is restless, unsteady, hard to control. The wise one makes it straight, like a fletcher straightens an arrow." Buddha also made it clear that mere external asceticism, or physical discipline, does not in itself lead to enlightenment: "What good is matted hair to you, idiot? What good is hide clothing? While your inward state is a tangle, you polish your exterior."[64]

The importance of a *true* teacher, a guide external to one's subjective imaginations, wishes and expectations, was emphasized by both Tantric Siddhas and Zen masters. They even abandoned the institutionalization of forms when this obstructed the perception of truth and truthfulness.

According to the famous Taoist wizard called Ancestor Lu, who is associated with amalgamating Taoism with Zen, "If you do away with writings but still stick to a teacher's tradition, this very teacher's tradition becomes a source of obstruction. You should by all means examine clearly and go to visit adepts who can transmit the profound marvel. If you don't find such a person, you will suffer from obstruction all your life.

"Generally speaking, beginners have dreams about the Way; once they make a mistake in choosing a teacher and are given false teachings, they are confused and cannot attain enlightenment. They follow false teachings all their lives, thinking them to be true guidance. Their bodies and minds become imprisoned, so that even if real people point out true awakening to them, they may repudiate it and turn away.

"Once they have tasted fanciful talk, they sell falsehood by falsehood, and believe falsehood through falsehood."[65]

Hold the rudder with a steady mind—
There's no other way to the other shore.

In the *Dhammapada,* Buddha says, "Like a fish out of water, cast on dry ground, this mind flops around trying to escape the realm of bedevilment.

"The mind is mercurial, hard to restrain, alighting where it wishes. It is good to master this mind; a disciplined mind brings happiness.

"Let the wise one watch over the mind, so hard to perceive, so artful, alighting where it wishes; a watchfully protected mind brings happiness.

"The mind travels afar, acts alone, is incorporeal, and haunts a cave; those who will control it escape the bonds of bedevilment."[66]

A boatman pulls a boat by a rope;
Give it up and go by naturalness alone.

The *Flower Ornament Scripture* says, "It is like a boat going to the ocean. Before it reaches the ocean, it is dragged with much effort, but once it reaches the ocean it is propelled without effort by the wind. The distance it travels on the ocean in one day is farther than it could be dragged by force in even a hundred years.

"In the same way, enlightening beings, having stored provisions of roots of goodness and boarded the ship of the Great Vehicle, reaching the great ocean of practice of enlightening beings, arrive at all-knowledge in a moment by effortless knowledge, which could not be reached even in countless eons by their former practices involving effort."[67]

There's terror on the road; brigands are strong.
All is told in the fluctuation of the world.

The Zen-Taoist wizard Ancestor Lu said, "The obstacle of bedevilment may arise in the mind, may attach to objects, may operate through other people, or may pertain to the body. Bedevilments arising in the mind are ideas of self and others, ideas of glory and ignominy, ideas of gain and loss, ideas of right and wrong, ideas of profit and honor, ideas of superiority. These are dust on the pedestal of the spirit, preventing freedom.

"Bedevilment in the body is when it is invaded by illness, hunger, cold, satiation, pain, and pleasure. When one becomes comfortable, one becomes lazy, repeating vicious circles into which one becomes trapped and bound."[68]

To the shore, he goes upstream in the swift current: Saraha says, "It is proved in the sky."

The "swift current" is the flow of conditioned states, thoughts, and feelings. Going "upstream" in the current means transcending these states, thoughts, and feelings even in their very midst, not going along with the force of their momentum, but focusing on the "shore" of ultimate truth. The aim, at this point, is realization of emptiness, so the Siddha says that it is "proved in the sky."

36

SARAHA

When your mind is split by sleep,
it's your own fault.
Enjoying the instruction of the teacher,
how can you remain a vagrant?
Wondrous, the sky born of hum!
When you've taken a Bengali wife,
your conceptions are destroyed.
Mysterious, the illusion of being—
it shows others versus self;
This world is a bubble—in naturalness the self is empty.
Leaving the nectar, you've swallowed the poison;
control of mind comes from oneself.
By understanding what about my own people and
others may I put up with vicious in-laws?
Saraha says, "Better an empty cowpen—
what use have I for a vicious bull?
Destroying the world on my own,
I enjoy myself at will."

When your mind is split by sleep,
it's your own fault.
Enjoying the instruction of the teacher,
how can you remain a vagrant?

In the Zen Buddhist practice of koan meditation, and in the Pure Land Buddhist practice of incantation, it is necessary to reach continuity that is unbroken even by sleep, unification of mind not split even in sleep, before the breakthrough of satori (in Zen) or Rebirth (in the Pure Land) can take place. Not being interrupted or diverted by sleep does not mean sleeplessness; what it signals is the transition from deliberate effort to spontaneity.

When the mind is split by sleep, this indicates that the practice of concentration is still deliberate. When the work is internalized as a natural process, in contrast, sleep does not divert the mind. The Siddha says that when the mind is split it is "your own fault" because it is your own deliberate effort that is interrupted. This is somewhat subtle, and can be understood only through personal experience.

The image of the vagrant is from the *Saddharmapundarika-sutra* or Lotus Sutra, one of the major revelations of universalist Buddhism. The vagrant is the son of a wealthy man who leaves home and falls into poverty, becoming a migrant laborer. When at last he is reunited with his father, the son does not recognize him. Only after employing his son and testing him for probity does the father at last reveal his identity and finally bequeath all his wealth to his son.

The father in this story represents the Buddha-nature, which the scripture declares is the original endowment inherent in everyone. The wanderings of the son represent the confusion into which the mind, unaware of its inherent Buddha-nature, falls. When the son returns and is employed on his father's estate, this represents exertion of effort in practice. When the father reveals their relationship and bequeaths his fortune to his son, this represents return to the original natural Buddha-nature and the realization of awakening.

In Zen Buddhism, the image of the vagrant as a migrant laborer is often used to represent those who try to attain enlightenment by subjectively motivated striving, ignorant of the intrinsic Buddha- nature. Here the Siddha presents an analogous image, again emphasizing the transition from deliberateness to spontaneity.

Wondrous, the sky born of hum!
When you've taken a Bengali wife,
your conceptions are destroyed.

The mantric syllable *hum* is the "seed letter" of the Buddha Akshobhya, whose name means "Immovable." According to the Ten Stages teaching of the *Flower Ornament Scripture,* immovability is attained in the eighth stage, which is the stage at which the practitioner transcends effort to attain effortlessness. Thus the Siddha artfully continues his teaching on spontaneity.

The *Flower Ornament Scripture* says, "As soon as they attain the eighth stage, Immovability, enlightening beings become freed from all efforts and attain the state of effortlessness, freed from physical, verbal, and mental striving, freed from stirring cogitation and flowing thoughts, and become stabilized in a natural state of development."[69] It also describes those in this state as "wholly detached from mind, intellect, consciousness, thought, and ideation. Unattached, not grasping, equal to space, having entered into the nature of openness." Such is the "wondrous (inconceivable) sky born of *hum.*"

The "Bengali wife" is another symbol of emptiness. As explained earlier, in Tantric Buddhism the wife ordinarily stands for *shunyata,* or emptiness, while the husband ordinarily stands for *upaya,* or method. Bengal was not culturally Hinduized or Sanskritized until comparatively late in its history, and even then never completely. This was the homeland of many Tantric adepts, and may have indeed been the original homeland of Tantric Buddhism.

The name Sanskrit, used for the cultivated language of Hinduism, means "compounded," and therefore is a convenient symbol for artificial convention, in the usage of those not socially and intellectually dominated by Sanskrit culture. Gautama Buddha himself, whose native Magadhi language was a forerunner of the Bengali language used by the Vajrayana Siddhas in these songs, was one of the first to abandon the ritual constrictions of Sanskrit language and Hindu cultural convention. If we understand "emptiness" as a window to reality beyond artificial conventions of thought and perception, "Bengali" is thus a marvelously apt symbol of the "culture" or "homeland" of the "wife" that is *shunyata,* "departure from all views."

Mysterious, the illusion of being—
it shows others versus self;
This world is a bubble—in naturalness the self is empty.

The illusion of others versus self refers to ignorance of the fact that the totality of all living beings is one single being, one single organism. It also refers to the artificial division between subject and object, created by the projection of subjective discriminations which are then reified as independent objective realities.

Buddhist teachings often refer to the world, including the empirical self, as like a bubble. This is said in view of its transitory, evanescent, insubstantial nature. But there is also more to this image. The *Shurangama-sutra* says, "Space is born within great awareness, like a bubble from the ocean." Here, "space" means that which contains the universe. The classical Zen master Pai-chang said, "Space is symbolized by the bubble; the ocean represents essence. The essence of inherent radiant awareness is greater than space, and so it is said that space is born within great awareness like a bubble from the ocean."

Since the self, here meaning the acquired psychological self, is a mental construct, its artificial boundaries dissolve in the state of naturalness, or effortless spontaneity. This is realized through the "inherent radiant awareness" of which Zen master Pai-chang speaks.

Leaving the nectar, you've swallowed the poison;
control of mind comes from oneself.
By understanding what about my own people and
others may I put up with vicious in-laws?

The teaching of emptiness is traditionally said to be both nectar and poison. It is nectar when it is accurately understood and thus releases the mind from bondage. It is poison when it is misconstrued and thereby leads to nihilism, antinomianism, or schizoid reification of "emptiness" as something apart from existence.

Zen master Pai-chang said, "The universally equal teaching of the Mahayana is like nectar, and also like poison. If you can digest it, it is like nectar; but if you cannot digest it, it is like poison. When reading scriptures and studying the teachings, if you do not understand the living word and the dead word, you will certainly not penetrate the meanings and expressions in them."

The Indian master Nagarjuna, considered the ancestor of both Zen and Vajrayana, wrote, "Emptiness seen wrongly destroys the weak-minded, like a mishandled snake or a misperformed spell."

The true teaching of emptiness, correctly understood and realized in actual experience, is the understanding that enables one to tolerate others, even the vicious, and their illusions, without self-righteousness. The *Flower Ornament Scripture* says, "Enlightening beings are able to see the things of the world this way: all things, existent and nonexistent, they realize are illusions; living beings and lands are made by various actions. Entering the realm of illusion, they have no attachment therein; thus attaining skillfulness, they are tranquil, free from folly."[70]

The same scripture also says of this understanding, "Realizing the world is empty, they do not destroy the things of the world."

Saraha says, "Better an empty cowpen—
what use have I for a vicious bull?
Destroying the world on my own,

I enjoy myself at will."

"Better an empty cowpen than a vicious bull" means that it is better not to grasp anything than to mistake something relative for an absolute. As usual in this literature, the female, here the "cow," represents emptiness, while the male, here the "bull," represents method, "skill in means." If religious forms are perverted to serve egotistic ambitions ("vicious bull"), as often happens in cultic movements and religious politics, it is better to have nothing to do with them at all.

Thus the Siddha speaks of "destroying the world," realizing emptiness, the absolute truth transcending all worldly concepts, "on my own," outside the realm of mundane establishments posing as religious bodies. In this way one attains personal experience of liberation, "enjoying myself at will," rather than becoming more entangled and fettered than ever by submitting to authoritarian institutions. And this is what the original Tantric adepts actually did.

37

KAHNU

For one whose mind-field is rubbish and junk,
The Tantric works are a necklace of bricks.
Say, how can nature be told of,
Where body, speech, and mind do not enter?
In vain does a guru teach a disciple;
How can what is beyond speech be told?
As much talk, so much rubbish;
The teacher is dumb, the student is deaf.
How can Kahnu tell of the winner's treasure?
As the deaf and dumb understand.

For one whose mind-field is rubbish and junk,
The Tantric works are a necklace of bricks.

If the mind is full of garbage, like desire for recognition, desire for power over others, desire for ascendancy, desire for self-esteem, or even simple thrill-seeking, religious practice only exaggerates these negative characteristics. Zen master Pai-chang said, "The world that is bound becomes and decays, but what the power of concentration holds will leak out to another realm, totally unawares."

Say, how can nature be told of,
Where body, speech, and mind do not enter?

This is another warning for those who are attached to ritual, doctrine, and meditation in the very same manner as attachment to any mundane thing. Pai-chang said, "How can you carve and polish emptiness to make an image of Buddha? How can you say emptiness is blue, yellow, red, or white? As it is said, 'Reality has no comparison, because there is nothing to which it may be likened; the embodiment of reality is not constructed and does not fall within the scope of any classification.' That is why it is said, 'The essence of the sage is nameless and cannot be spoken; it is impossible to linger in the empty door of truth as it really is.' Just as insects can alight anywhere but the flames of a fire, people's minds can relate to anything but transcendental insight."

In vain does a guru teach a disciple;
How can what is beyond speech be told?

Pai -chang said, "When you call on teachers to seek some knowledge or understanding, this is the demon of 'teachers,' because it gives rise to verbalization and opinion." He also said, "Just detach from all sound and form, and do not dwell in detachment either; and do not dwell in intellectual understanding. This is practice."

As much talk, so much rubbish;
The teacher is dumb, the student is deaf.

Pai-chang said, "If one should say, 'I am capable of explaining, I am able to understand; I am the teacher, you are the disciple,' this is the same as demonic suggestion." Zen master Yuansou said, "There is no real doctrine at all for you to chew on or squat over. If you will not believe in yourself, you pick up your baggage and go around to other people's houses looking for Zen, looking for the Way, looking for mysteries, looking for marvels, looking for Buddhas, looking for Zen masters, looking for teachers."[71]

How can Kahnu tell of the winner's treasure?
As the deaf and dumb understand.

Zen master Ju-ching said, "You must strip off your eyes so that you see nothing at all; then after that, there is nothing you don't see. . . . You must block your ears shut so that you hear nothing at all; then after that, there is nothing you don't hear."

In *The Blue Cliff Record,* Zen master Yuan-wu says, "Even if your whole body were an eye, you still wouldn't be able to see It. Even if your whole body were an ear, you still wouldn't be able to hear It. Even if your whole body were a mouth, you still wouldn't be able to speak of It. Even if your whole body were a mind, you still wouldn't be able to perceive It.

"Now, leaving aside 'whole body' for the moment, if you had no eyes, how would you see? Without ears, how would you hear? Without a mouth, how would you speak? Without a mind, how would you perceive? If you can unfurl a single pathway here, you'll be a fellow student with the ancient Buddhas."[72]

38

BHUSUKU

This world is nonexistent from the start;
it appears to be by mistake.
How can one who is startled by the rope-snake
be bitten by the fiber rope in reality?
Wondrous Yogi, don't dirty your hands!
With such behavior, if you are awake in the world,
your habitual desires will fall away.
It is like a mirage, a fairy city,
a reflection in a mirror—
In the midst of the whirlwind,
be yourself firm as a rock.
Like the son of a sterile woman
playing many kinds of sports,
Space is swollen by oil from sand,
by the horns of a hare.
The Warrior says clearly, Bhusuku says clearly,
"All is such of its own nature:
If you are ignorant and confused,
ask a teacher of truth and find out."

This world is nonexistent from the start;
it appears to be by mistake.

How can one who is startled by the rope-snake be bitten by the fiber rope in reality?

In terms of the metaphysics of Buddhist Yoga, to which this couplet overtly refers, "this world" means the world as we represent it to ourselves in our thoughts, according to conditioned mental predilections and habits. In technical Sanskrit, this is called the *parikalpita-svabhava,* or the nature of things as conceptualized. This projected nature of things is traditionally symbolized by the fearful misperception of a length of rope as a snake. Pursuing this illustration, the "rope" stands for *paratantra-svabhava,* the dependent nature of things. The fact that the rope is not a rope of itself, but a bundle of fibers, is called the *parinishpanna-svabhava,* the perfect, absolute, or real nature of things.

The *Sandhinirmocana-sutra,* a classic of Buddhist Yoga, explains, "People produce explanations of the dependent and real natures based on the characteristics of the conceptualized nature, saying they are such and such, in accord with how people conceptualize them. Because the explanations condition their minds, because their awareness conforms to the explanations, because they are lulled by the explanation, they cling to their conceptualizations."[73]

The comprehensive pan-Buddhist *Flower Ornament Scripture* illustrates this principle by the image of the mind as an artist. Mistaking the conceptualized nature of things for objective reality is delusion. Zen master Pai-chang Cheng wrote, "An artist draws a picture of hell, depicting hundreds and thousands of scenes; setting down his brush, he looks it over, and feels a shiver run through him." The scripture says, "Of all things seen in the world, only mind is the host; by grasping forms according to interpretation it becomes deluded, not true to reality."

According to an ancient story frequently alluded to in Chinese Zen teachings to explain the significance of this point, once a man at a banquet lifted his wine goblet and saw in it the reflection of a bow hanging on the wall behind him. Mistaking it for a little snake in the wine, yet unable to stop his momentum, he went ahead and drank the wine; then he became sickened, thinking he had swallowed a viper. Later, when he saw the bow on the wall and realized what had really happened, he knew the "snake" was a product of his own imagination, and immediately recovered his health.

Wondrous Yogi, don't dirty your hands!
With such behavior, if you are awake in the world,
your habitual desires will fall away.

To "dirty your hands" means grasping and clinging to illusions and delusions. Zen master K'en-t'ang wrote, "In a village where the wells are poisoned, the water should not even be tasted; with even a single drop, the whole family dies."

"If you are awake in the world" indicates that nonattachment, not "dirtying your hands," does not mean escapism or nihilism, but understanding the real nature of the world. Zen master Wu-men wrote, "If no idle matters hang on your mind, then it is a good season in the human world."[74]

With this realization, habitual desires "fall away" even while in the world, because they are rooted in subjectivity, not in objectivity. Zen master Dogen wrote, "Minding already gone, 'mindless' does not quite describe it. In this life, purity is foremost."[75]

It is like a mirage, a fairy city,
a reflection in a mirror—
In the midst of the whirlwind,
be yourself firm as a rock.

The *Flower Ornament Scripture* says, "The world is like a mirage, differentiated because of conceptions; knowing the world is ideation, one is freed from delusions of thought, view, and mind. Just as people think a mirage in the heat is water, yet the water does not exist and the wise should not seek it, the same is true of sentient beings: worldly states are all nonexistent, like mirages, existing in the perception—this is the realm of the unobstructed mind."[76] Zen master Dogen wrote, "The autumn colors of the thousand peaks are dyed with seasonal rain; how could the hard rock on the mountain follow along with the wind?"[77]

Like the son of a sterile woman
playing many kinds of sports,
Space is swollen by oil from sand,
by the horns of a hare.

The son of a sterile woman, oil pressed from sand, and the horns of a hare, are all images commonly used in Zen as well as Tantric Buddhism. They do not represent absolute nonexistence, or illogic or irrationality, as has been claimed by misguided Zen popularizers; they symbolize the identity of true emptiness and inconceivable existence. The *Flower Ornament Scripture* says, "Enlightening beings examine all things, clearly realize all are like phantoms, and carry out phantomlike practice, never giving it up. . . . Buddhas liberate phantom beings with great kindness and compassion. The liberation is also phantomlike; they teach them by phantom power."[78]

The Warrior says clearly, Bhusuku says clearly,
"All is such of its own nature:
If you are ignorant and confused,
ask a teacher of truth and find out."

Zen master Fen-yang wrote, "Few believe in the Buddha in their own mind; unwilling to take responsiblity for it, they suffer a lot of cramps. Arbitrary ideas, greed and anger, the wrappings of afflictions, all are conditioned on attachment to the cave of ignorance."[79]

Zen master Fo-yen said, "The Way is not only evident after explanation and demonstration, because it is always being revealed naturally. Explanation and demonstration are expedients used to enable you to realize intuitive understanding; they are only temporary byways. Whether you attain realization through explanation, or enter in through demonstration, or reach the goal by spontaneous sensing through individual awareness, ultimately there is no different thing or separate attainment. It is just a matter of reaching the source of mind."[80]

39

KAHNU

Emptiness is filled by the nature of mind;
Don't be saddened by detachment from the clusters.
How can you say Kahnu is not there?
Day by day he penetrates the triple world.
The ignorant one is distressed
on seeing the perishing of what is seen,
But how can a broken wave make the ocean run dry?
Being ignorant, people do not look closely—
They do not see the cream there within the milk.
No one who leaves the world comes back here;
Kahnu the Yogi revels in such an existence.

Emptiness is filled by the nature of mind;
Don't be saddened by detachment from the clusters.

This couplet emphasizes the perennial insistence that "emptiness," in Buddhist usage, is a technical term and is not meant in the ordinary literal sense of absence, nonexistence, or removal of something existent. The "clusters" are the components of the mortal being, as traditionally defined in Buddhist practical philosophy: form, sensation, conception, synergy, and consciousness. Not being "saddened by detachment from the clusters" means realizing that detachment from transitory things, in Buddhist practice, is not based on nihilistic rejection but on the emptiness of absoluteness; so nothing real is destroyed in the process; nothing is lost, except delusion.

How can you say Kahnu is not there?
Day by day he penetrates the triple world.

This couplet emphasizes the pragmatic implications of the principle that realization of emptiness and nonattachment, in the Buddhist sense, does not mean, and does not lead to nihilism or quietism. Zen master Pai-chang said, "Buddhahood is not inactivity; it is not passivity, or quiescence in the darkness." Pai-chang also said, "Cultivating mundane causes while in the sanctified state, a Buddha enters among sentient beings, becoming like them in kind to invite, lead, teach, and guide them. Joining those hungry spirits, limbs and joints afire, one expounds transcendental wisdom to them, inspiring them with the will for enlightenment. If one just remained in the sanctified state, how could one go there and talk with them?

"Buddha enters into various classes and makes a raft for sentient beings; like them, he feels pain, unlimited toil and stress. When a Buddha enters a painful place, he too feels pain, the same as sentient beings. A Buddha is not the same as sentient beings only in that he is free to go or to stay."

The ignorant one is distressed
on seeing the perishing of what is seen,
But how can a broken wave make the ocean run dry?

The mind constricted by discriminatory thinking sees persons and things as isolated existences in themselves, rather than as part of a totality comprising all beings and things. By shifting attention to the totality, in contrast, one sees that a "broken wave," an isolated individual, event, or phenomenon, which arises and passes away, is part of an "ocean" of universal interdependence. The former mode of consciousness is called the aspect of mind that is born and dies; the latter is called the aspect of mind that is true to suchness.

Being ignorant, people do not look closely—
They do not see the cream there within the milk.

In terms of phenomena, the "milk" here refers to external appearances, while the "cream" refers to inner essence. In terms of mind, the "milk" refers to conditioned consciousness, while the "cream" refers to the essence of consciousness. Cream within milk means Buddha-nature within the human mind.

No one who leaves the world comes back here;
Kahnu the Yogi revels in such an existence.

Zen master Hua-yen was asked, "How is it when greatly enlightened people return to confusion?"

The Zen master replied, "A broken mirror does not shine again; fallen leaves cannot climb up a tree."

Zen master Dogen wrote:

The wind is still throughout the world,
birds cry, the mountains are quiet.

The crossroads are bright as daybreak,
the doors of the senses cool as autumn.
Half sitting where there is no doubt,
one sees illusion in a floating reflection.[81]

40

BHUSUKU

The tree of nature pervades the triple world;
O space-like intrinsic essence,
who is released from caste?
Just as drinking water spilled into water
cannot be distinguished,
So does the mind-jewel merge into the sky.
Where there is no self, how can there be other?
The origin nonexistent,
birth and death have no being.
Bhusuku says, "Wondrous!"
The Warrior says, "Wondrous!" All is essentially thus!
Going and not coming back,
therein is neither being nor nonbeing.

The tree of nature pervades the triple world;
O space-like intrinsic essence,
who is released from caste?

The triple world—consisting of the realm of desire, the realm of form, and the formless realm—is by nature empty of instrinsic essence or absolute reality. There is no exception to emptiness in all the world, but the nonexistence of absoluteness does not erase the existence of relativity. Indeed, they are one and the same—relativity *is* emptiness. The great master Nagarjuna, ancestor of both Zen and Tantric Buddhism, wrote in his seminal verses on the Middle Way, *yah pratityasamutpadah sunyatam tam pracaksmahe,* "Interdependent origination, we declare, is itself emptiness."

For this reason, even though Buddhism is casteless, and the original Tantric movement went further than any other form of Buddhism in overcoming or breaking through the tyranny of caste prejudice, especially in Bengal, yet caste divisions were generally maintained socially and politically by Hindu power structures; nevertheless realized Buddhists were psychologically and spiritually freed by their inner understanding.

This spiritual realization is concentrated in the question "Who is released?" This encapsulation is not simply an allusion to selflessness (the ultimate unreality of the secondary, psychologically and socio-culturally conditioned ego); it is a meditation exercise, looking into the innermost essence of mind. This is what Zen Buddhists call "turning the light around and looking back," which is also part of the old Tibetan practice of Mahamudra, the Great Symbol.

Just as drinking water spilled into water
cannot be distinguished,
So does the mind-jewel merge into the sky.

The "mind merging with the sky" refers to the practice and realization that Zen-inspired neo-Taoists call "absolute nonresistance." The Taoist master known as Preserver of Truth said, "In the beginning of study of the Way, it is necessary to sit calmly, collect the mind, and detach from objects, so the mind does not possess anything. By dwelling in nonpossessiveness, one does not cling to anything, spontaneously entering into absolute nonresistance. The mind then merges with the Way."[82]

This type of practice also has precedent in ancient classical Taoism, as noted in the book of the Huainan Masters: "What sages learn is to return their nature to the beginning, and let the mind travel freely in openness. What developed people learn is to link their nature to vast emptiness and become aware of the silent infinite."[83]

Where there is no self, how can there be other?
The origin nonexistent,
birth and death have no being.

The 17th-century Zen master Bankei said, "If you don't think of being superior to others, you won't be inferior to them."

A common Buddhist dictum often quoted in Zen texts says, "When the mind is excited, all things arise; when the mind is quiet, all things quiesce." The third patriarch of Zen wrote, "When the one mind does not conceive, all things are error-free."

The *Blue Cliff Record* poses the question, "Right now, where do seeing and not seeing, hearing and not hearing, speaking and not speaking, knowing and not knowing, come from?" This is not a rhetorical or philosophical question, but a meditation exercise. The Taoist master called Preserver of Truth said, "Concentrating on the absolute, practice being unborn."[84]

This exercise also has its precedent in classical Taoism, according to the Huainan Masters: "Sages send the spirit to the capital of awareness and return to the beginning of myriad things. They look at the formless and listen to the soundless. In the midst of profound darkness, they alone see light; in the midst of silent vastness, they alone have illumination."[85]

Bhusuku says, "Wondrous!"
The Warrior says, "Wondrous!" All is essentially thus!
Going and not coming back,
therein is neither being nor nonbeing.

The term *arhat,* used for a Buddhist saint who has overcome the world and attained nirvana, is sometimes interpreted as deriving from *ari-han,* "killer of the enemy." The image of the warrior, who fights egoism and delusion, is common in Buddhist texts. Here, the Siddha Bhusuku is referring to himself.

In the *Sandhinirmocana-sutra,* "one-pointedness of mind" is defined as "realizing that images concentrated on are only consciousness; or, realizing this, to meditate on suchness." The statement that "all is essentially thus" means seeing things as they really are, undistorted by subjective projections based on conditioned conceptualizations.

"Going and not coming back" refers to "departure from all views," as Nagarjuna has defined emptiness, leaving behind all biased notions; and because emptiness is relativity, here there is neither absolute being nor absolute nonbeing. Such is the transcendent Middle Way.

41

KANKANA

When the void joins the void,
All things then arise.
I am perfectly aware of the four moments;
By stopping in between, there is supreme awakening.
Dot and crescent have not entered the mind;
While seeking one, the other's lost.
Knowing where you come from,
You remain centered, totally unencumbered.
Kankana says, in tumultuous. sounds,
"All has been smashed by the roar of suchness!"

When the void joins the void,
All things then arise.

The two "voids" are mind and objects. When the mind is empty of preconceptions and sees actuality void of subjective projections, everything is *suchness.* The *Flower Ornament Scripture* says, "No view is seeing that can see all things. If one has views about things, this is not seeing anything." It also says, "People wrongly conceptualize things spoken of in conventional terms; knowing the world is all birthless, this is seeing the world."

I am perfectly aware of the four moments;
By stopping in between, there is supreme awakening.

The "four moments" are the moment before a thought arises, the moment of imminent arising, the moment of actual arising, and the moment of passing away. Mindfulness of these four moments is the basis of one of the meditation practices of T'ien-t'ai Buddhism, among the parent schools of Zen. "Stopping in between" means not dwelling on any of these moments, even while aware of them. By this technique, the extra dimensions of consciousness that are beyond thought per se become accessible. The classical Zen master Ma-tsu said, "When successive thoughts do not await each other, and thought after thought dies out moment to moment, this is called the oceanic meditation. It takes in all truths, just as hundreds of thousands of different streams all return to the ocean."

Dot and crescent have not entered the mind;
While seeking one, the other's lost.

Dot and crescent stand for sun and moon, which represent the absolute and relative thought of enlightenment. This couplet alludes to the state of realization, transcending aspiration. If one focuses only on the absolute, one becomes oblivious to the relative; if one focuses only on the relative, one has no sense of the absolute.

According to a koan in the classic collection *Annals of the Empty Valley,* Zen master Ch'ing-yuan asked the illustrious Sixth Patriarch of Zen, who was famous for the natural wisdom known in Zen as teacherless knowledge, "What should be done to avoid falling into stages?" The Patriarch asked back, "What have you done?" Ch'ing-yuan said, "I don't even practice the holy truths." The Patriarch retorted, "Then what stage do you fall into?" Ch'ing-yuan said, "Since I don't even practice the holy truths, what stage would I fall into?" The Patriarch said, "Right! Keep it well."

Remarking on this, the later master Pao-en said, "Utterly forgetting human convention, what's the need of second thoughts? Shattering the mass of doubt, how does it require a single remark? Who is the one who finds the marvel free in all ways, not lingering in the mystic gate?" This bespeaks the realization to which the Bengali Siddha Kankana alludes in this couplet.

Knowing where you come from,
You remain centered, totally unencumbered.

Ma-tsu said, "The triple world is only mind; all forms are impressions of a single truth. Whatever form you see, you are seeing mind. Mind is not mind of itself; there is mind because of form. . . . What is born in the mind is called form; when you know that form is empty, then birth is unborn. If you understand this mind, then you can dress and eat according to the times, nurturing the embryo of sagehood. What further concern is there?"

The Second Patriarch of Zen asked the Founder of Zen, "My mind is not at peace; please give me peace of mind." The Founder replied, "Bring me your mind, and I will make it peaceful." The Second Patriarch said, "When I search for my mind, I cannot find it." The Founder said, "I have pacified your mind."

The *Diamond Cutting Wisdom Scripture* says, "Past mind cannot be grasped, future mind cannot be grasped, present mind cannot be grasped."

The *Flower Ornament Scripture* says, "Mind discriminates worlds, but that mind has no existence. The enlightened know this truth, and thus see the body of Buddha."[86] It also says, "No view is called seeing, the birthless is called beings. Whether views or beings, knowing they've no substantial nature, the seer dismisses entirely the subject and object of seeing; not destroying reality, this person knows the Buddha."[87]

Kankana says, in tumultuous. sounds,
"All has been smashed by the roar of suchness!"

Smashing everything by the roar of suchness means realizing what is referred to in Buddhist Yoga as the "selflessness of things in true suchness." The selflessness of things means there is no inherent identity in things, as their definitions and identities are actually projected mental constructions.

The *Flower Ornament Scripture* says, "If one can know this real body's quiescent character of true thusness, one can see the truly enlightened transcending the path of speech. Things expressed in words cannot disclose the character of reality; only through equanimity can one see things, including the Buddha."[88]

The same scripture says, "There is no creator or created; they only arise from habitual conceptions. How can we know it is so? Because other than this, naught is. All things have no abode; no definite locus can be found. The Buddhas abide in this, ultimately unwavering."[89]

42

KAHNU

The mind is a tree, the five senses its branches:
Desires are its plentiful leaves and fruits.
He cuts with the axe of a supreme teacher's words;
Kahnu says, "The tree won't grow again!"
Pure and impure water make the tree grow;
The wise one who obeys the teacher cuts it.
The fool who knows not to cut or split the tree
Accepts its existence
even when it's rotted and fallen.
Void is the tree at its best, space the axe:
Cut the tree, so that the root does not sprout.

The mind is a tree, the five senses its branches:
Desires are its plentiful leaves and fruits.

Zen master Lan-hsi wrote, "Ordinary people are like trees: putting the manure of greed and lust on the thin soil of folly and delusion, planting seeds of ignorance, transplanting shoots of the five clusters; they produce buds of habit-ridden consciousness, growing roots of attachment and stems of egoism toward others, bringing forth branches of flattery and deceit, sprouting leaves of jealousy and envy, creating trees of affliction, causing the flowers of infatuation to bloom, forming fruits of the three poisons of craving, antagonism, and stupidity. When the tasks of name and gain are done, they sing the songs of desires."

He cuts with the axe of a supreme teacher's words;
Kahnu says, "The tree won't grow again!"

Once upon a time there were seven princesses, known as the Seven Sagacious Women. One day, on the occasion of a seasonal flower festival, when great crowds of people were hurrying to the parks to enjoy themselves, one of the Seven Sagacious Women said to the others, "We should not go along like everyone else to frolic in the realm of the senses for mundane pleasures. We should go to the forest of corpses."

The other women said, "There are corpses rotting everywhere there; what is good about that?"

The first woman said, "Let's just go; there will be something good."

When they got to the forest, the woman pointed to a corpse and asked the other women, "The corpse is here; where has the person gone?"

Reflecting on this, the women all attained enlightenment.

Pure and impure water make the tree grow;
The wise one who obeys the teacher cuts it.

According to Zen master Pai-chang, the introductory teaching of Buddhism is for "weeding out impure things," while the advanced teaching is for "weeding out pure things." He explains, "When traces do not appear on either side, then there is neither lack nor sufficiency, neither profane nor holy, neither light nor dark. This is not having knowledge, yet not lacking knowledge; it is not bondage, not liberation."

Obsession with "pure things" can delude people even more deeply than attachment to "impure things," because of the blinding demon of self-righteousness. Pai-chang also said, "Just do not be affected by greed for anything, even being or nonbeing. When it comes to the matter of untying bonds, there are no special words or phrases to teach people. If you say there are some particular verbal expressions to teach people, or that there is some particular doctrine to give people, this is called heresy and demonic suggestion."

Pai-chang further describes spiritual progress in terms of successive attachments and detachments, ultimately transcending obsession with both impure things and pure things: "To dwell on evil when encountering evil is called the enlightenment of sentient beings. To dwell on goodness when encountering goodness is called the enlightenment of Buddhist disciples. Not dwelling on either side, good or bad, and yet not making nondwelling an understanding, is called the enlightenment of bodhisattvas. Only when you neither dwell on anything nor make an understanding of nondwelling can this finally be called the enlightenment of Buddhas."

The fool who knows not to cut or split the tree
Accepts its existence
even when it's rotted and fallen.

One who does not know how to analyze the body to overcome gross self-centered obsession with sensation and emotional experience clings to self-importance even in the face of undeniable evidence of fragility and mortality.

Void is the tree at its best, space the axe:
Cut the tree, so that the root does not sprout.

Lan-hsi wrote, "Is there anyone who can pull the tree out by the roots with a single hand, and plant it on a ground where there is neither light nor shade, making a shadowless tree? This must be someone with great power, who has the same root as heaven and earth, the same body as all things."

Zen master Dogen said, "Having pruned away the tree on the moon, tonight I don't long for any tonight of yore. When a foreigner comes, a foreigner is reflected; when a native comes, a native. This is the boundless pure light of the full moon night."[90]

JAYANANDI

Like a mirror looked at in dreams,
So the delusion that intervenes.
When the mind is freed of delusion,
Then comings and goings are gone.
It is not to be burned, nor soaked, nor cut off;
See how illusion recurs in delusion again and again.
The body is like a shadow illusion;
It is beyond the two extremes.
Suchness of mind is inherently pure;
Jayanandi says directly, "There is no other."

Like a mirror looked at in dreams,
So the delusion that intervenes.

The mirror looked at in dreams symbolizes arbitrary subjectivity unconnected to objective reality. What this mirror reflects is conditioned mental habit, the predilections and preoccupations of the self, constructing pictures from bits of stored impressions. The projections of subjective bias, mistaken for objective realities, are delusions that screen the mind from truth. In the words of a Buddhist proverb often quoted in Chinese Zen, "Cataracts in the eye make flowers in the sky."

When the mind is freed of delusion,
Then comings and goings are gone.

The eighth-century Zen master Ma-tsu said, "True suchness of mind is like a clear mirror reflecting forms. The mirror represents the mind; the forms represent all things. If the mind grasps at things, it gets involved in external conditions; this is the meaning of birth and death. If the mind does not grasp at things, this is the meaning of true suchness."

He also said, "The path does not require cultivation; just do not be polluted. What is pollution? As long as you have a mind that is born and dies, with artificial contrivance, all of it is pollution. If you want to realize the path directly, the normal mind is the path. What is the normal mind? It has no artificiality, no affirmation, no grasping or rejection, no nihilism or eternalism, no profanity or holiness." This approach to enlightenment is just like the *sahaja* or "natural" path of the Bengali adepts.

The *Flower Ornament Scripture* says, "Having risen above all views, whether mundane or transcendental, yet able to know the truth, one becomes a great illuminate."

It is not to be burned, nor soaked, nor cut off;
See how illusion recurs in delusion again and again.

Illusion cannot be "burned, soaked, or cut off" precisely because it is illusory and not actually real. On the persistent habit of entertaining illusions about delusions, the *Flower Ornament Scripture* says, "Ignorant creatures, because of continually slipping into erroneous views, because of minds shrouded by the darkness of ignorance, because of being puffed up with pride, because of conceptions, because of mental fixations of desires caught in the web of craving, because of hopes pursued by actions in the tangle of deceit and falsehood, because of deeds connected with envy and jealousy producing mundane states, because of accumulation of actions rife with passion, hatred, and folly, because of the flames of mind ignited by anger and resentment, because of undertaking of actions bound up with delusion, because of seeds in the mind, intellect, and consciousness bound to the flows of lust, existence, and ignorance, therefore produce sprouts of subsequent mundane life."[91]

The body is like a shadow illusion;
It is beyond the two extremes.

The two extremes are being and nonbeing; illusion neither exists nor does not exist. It does not exist absolutely, but it does exist mentally. The *Flower Ornament Scripture* says, "When great enlightening beings see all worlds as like illusions, they do not see beings born or dying, they do not see countries born or passing away, they do not see phenomena born or perishing."[92]

It further explains, "The world is like a mirage, differentiated because of conceptions; knowing the world is ideation, one is freed from delusions of thought, view, and mind."[93]

Suchness of mind is inherently pure;
Jayanandi says directly, "There is no other."

The *Sandhinirmocana-sutra* says, "With supremely pure awareness, the Buddha was attached neither to the mundane nor the supramundane. He proceeded according to formless truth and dwelt in the abode of the enlightened ones. He had arrived at equality with all the enlightened ones and had reached the point of nonobstruction and the state of unchangeability."[94]

The Zen master Hsia-t'ang said, "'Buddha' is a temporary name for what cannot be seen when you look, what cannot be heard when you listen, whose place of origin and passing away cannot be found when you search. It covers sound and form, pervades sky and earth, penetrates above and below. There is no second view, no second person, no second thought. It is everywhere, in everything, not something external. This is why the single source of awareness is called 'Buddha.'"[95]

44

DHARMA

Lotus and Lightning have become friends;
The outcaste woman's burned
in the yoga of equality.
The house of the Gypsy woman is afire;
Sprinkle water with the moon.
There are no scorching flames,
smoke does not appear;
By way of the highest peak, one enters into the sky.
The idols Vishnu, Shiva, and Brahma are burnt;
Nine times the royal grant deed's been burned.
Dharma says, "Clearly we know—
The water's risen in the five pipes."

Lotus and Lightning have become friends;
The outcaste woman's burned
in the yoga of equality.

Lotus and lightning stand for emptiness and compassion, insight and skill in means, represented as female and male. The harmonious combination of emptiness and compassion, the integration of insight and skill in means, characterizes the realization of Buddhist enlightenment. In these terms, the burning of the outcaste woman (emptiness) in the yoga (union) of equality refers to the realization of emptiness as the essential nature of being, not as an independent or isolated "void" existing of itself.

In terms of Tantric sexual yoga, the friendship of lotus and lightning symbolizes the union of female and male. In this context, the "outcaste woman" represents the central channel of the esoteric energy body visualized in meditation, the channel of purification. The "burning" stands for the blazing of the bliss of climactic sexually generated energy. This burns away the conceptual complications that ordinarily clutter the conditioned consciousness. This "burning" takes place in "equality" in the sense that it makes the practitioner indifferent to transitory thoughts. It also means that in order to be effective for spiritual purposes, this practice must be based upon, and carried out in, a state of equanimity.

The house of the Gypsy woman is afire;
Sprinkle water with the moon.

The Gypsy woman, or washerwoman (dombi), symbolizes the cleared central channel of purification. The woman's house represents the body, and the physical world; on another level, it represents the psychic state of the central channel of the energy body. In terms of the house symbolizing the body and the physical world, the fact that the house is "afire" alludes to the impermanence of the body and the world. In terms of the internal symbolism, the house afire represents the central channel energized by the blaze of ecstasy.

The moon stands for the relative thought of enlightenment. To sprinkle water on the fire with the moon means, on the level of external symbolism, to realize the transitory nature of the body, its capacities, and the physical environment as a whole. This is the means of maintaining a balance of detachment in the midst of ecstatic bliss. On the level of internal symbolism, sprinkling water with the moon means inwardly realizing the relative nature of the experience of bliss, thus maintaining equanimity even in ecstasy.

In both esoteric and exoteric Buddhism, this gesture of balance is standard practice whenever there is opening of access to extraordinary experiences or capacities. This prevents psychological aberration and spiritual deterioration through instinctive grasping and exaltation of the ego.

There are no scorching flames,
smoke does not appear;
By way of the highest peak, one enters into the sky.

The absence of scorching flames and smoke alludes to maintenance of balanced equanimity and inward calmness in the midst of ecstasy. The highest peak represents orgasmic climax; entering this way into the sky means using this natural bliss to clear the mind of conceptual clingings and complications, including fantasy and longing, in order to perceive emptiness, as "departure from all views."

The idols Vishnu, Shiva, and Brahma are burnt;
Nine times the royal grant deed's been burned.

In psychological and spiritual terms, the burning of these idols refers to transcendence of concepts of destruction, subsistence, and creation. As the *Diamond Cutting Wisdom Scripture* says, "Past mind cannot be grasped, future mind cannot be grasped, present mind cannot be grasped."

The burning of the grant deed nine times symbolizes a ninestep process of transcending proprietary attachments. On one level of interpretation, the "nine times" refer to the classic nine stages of meditation, from the first stage, which is characterized by attention, examination, joy, bliss, and single-mindedness, through the ninth stage, which is characterized by cessation of all sensation and perception. Nirvana, in the Buddhist sense, is beyond this ninth stage; so the "grant deed" of proprietary attachment is "burned" nine times, symbolizing ultimate transcendence through and beyond these nine stages.

On another level of interpretation, the number nine derives from three times three, referring to entry, abiding, and exit of three stages—detachment, not abiding in detachment, and not making an understanding of nonabiding. In Zen terms, this is referred to as "nine pounds of tortoise hair," alluding to the nine stages as well as the ultimate transcendence.

Dharma says, "Clearly we know—
The water's risen in the five pipes."

The five pipes are the five basic senses; the water is conscious energy. "Clearly we know" alludes to awareness of the senses clarified by the purification process.

Zen master Dogen said, "Everyone holds a luminous jewel, all embosom a precious gem; if you do not turn your attention around and look within, you will wander from home with a hidden treasure. Have you not heard it said, 'In the ear, it is like the great and small sounds in an empty valley, none not complete; in the eye, it is like myriad images under a thousand suns, none able to avoid casting shadows'? If you seek it outside of sense experience, you will hinder the living meaning of Zen."[96]

As the order of these Tantric couplets by Dharma illustrates, this comes after clarification and purification. Zen master Dogen also said, alluding to the same caveat, "Unless the cold pierces through our bones once, how can we have the apricot blossoms perfuming the whole world?"[97]

45

BHUSUKU

Crossing over,
the diamond boat travels the lotus canal;
Afflictions have been carried away
by the Bengali Nonduality.
Today Bhusuku's become a Bengali,
Having taken an outcaste for his wife.
The five ports are burnt,
the realms of the senses destroyed:
I do not know where my mind has gone.
I've no more gold or silver;
Compassion to those around me remains.
I have appropriated the whole treasury;
There is no difference in living and dying.

Crossing over,
the diamond boat travels the lotus canal;
Afflictions have been carried away
by the Bengali Nonduality.

The diamond and lotus are the two universes of phenomena and noumena, formal knowledge and formless insight, compassion and wisdom. Their conjunction produces the completeness of enlightened experience.

The sexual symbolism of the boat and canal are obvious; the precondition of "crossing over" alludes to the aforementioned precondition of purification.

Bengali culture is a synthesis of non-Aryan and Aryan cultures; here this historical "Bengali Nonduality" symbolically represents union of emptiness and form, or absolute and relative truth, the quintessence of enlightenment.

Today Bhusuku's become a Bengali,
Having taken an outcaste for his wife.

Bhusuku, the man, symbolizes formal knowledge and skill in means; the outcaste wife symbolizes formless insight and emptiness. Becoming a Bengali represents synthesis of these two aspects of enlightenment in a completely integrated whole.

The five ports are burnt,
the realms of the senses destroyed:
I do not know where my mind has gone.

The five ports are the senses; burning symbolizes ecstasy, and resulting nonattachment. Destruction of the realms of the senses symbolizes transcendence of the senses; "I do not know where my mind has gone" alludes to transcendence of egocentric experience of the senses.

I've no more gold or silver;
Compassion to those around me remains.

Gold and silver represent the absolute and relative thought of enlightenment; these are means of orientation and practice. When enlightenment itself is fully realized, the thought of enlightenment is held no more; the means are relinquished on attainment of the end.

The compassion of the enlightened is called objectless or unconditional compassion; this means that the objects of this compassion are not selected by subjective design, or based on preconceived conditions. Thus it is spontaneous compassion; so the couplet does not say that it is exercised, but that it "remains."

I have appropriated the whole treasury;
There is no difference in living and dying.

The whole treasury is complete enlightenment, sometimes referred to in Buddhist literature as the land of jewels. That "there is no difference in living and dying" refers to realization of nonduality of samsara and nirvana. The *Flower Ornament Scripture* says, "Just as space never increases or decreases whether all worlds become or disintegrate, because space has no birth, similarly the enlightenment of Buddhas has no increase or decrease whether there is attainment of enlightenment or not, because enlightenment has no signs or countersigns, no unity and no variety." It also says, "Like birthlessness is the emergence of Buddha, like deathlessness the nirvana of Buddha: all words and similes end—all purposes are achieved, beyond compare."

46

SABARA

Void upon void; axe the third house with the mind.
The girl who is egolessness at heart
is well protected while awake.
Untie, release the vexatious knot
of illusion and delusion!
Frolicking in great ecstasy,
the Wild Man has taken the Void to wife.
Look here! My third house is like space!
How splendid! The cotton is in bloom!
Beside the third house is the moonlight;
Darkness opened, space blossoms.
The millet is ripened,
the wild man and woman are drunk;
All day long the savage feels naught,
senseless in great ecstasy.
The fourth abode is built of basketwork;
Hoisted up on it, the savage has been cremated,
while a virtuous she-jackal cries.
The one intoxicated with the world has died,
offering to the dead made in the ten directions;
Look—the savage has become inert,
his wildness at an end.

Void upon void; axe the third house with the mind.
The girl who is egolessness at heart
is well protected while awake.

Void upon void stands for the emptiness of emptiness, called *sunyata-sunyata* or *sunyata-atisunyata* in Sanskrit. This is the fourth emptiness in the *prajna-paramita* teaching.

The third house is thus the third emptiness, which is inner and outer emptiness, or emptiness of the internal and external. The fourth emptiness is used to "axe" or "empty" the experience to which the third emptiness alludes, resulting in more subtle and more completely integrating liberation and enlightenment.

Nagarjuna, the specialist on emptiness, wrote that "ultimate truth cannot be expressed without resorting to conventional usage; nirvana cannot be attained without arriving at ultimate truth." In resorting to conventional usage, Tantric Buddhism may use concepts or terminology of Hinduism or other religions. This gives some the impression of syncretism, but in its genuine form it is actually pure Buddhism, in the act of applying this particular principle.

In the context of multifaceted Bengal, use of selected Hindu structures would be normal for Tantric Buddhists. Pursuing this potential in the interpretation of this couplet, the "third house" would be the third stage of life, enjoyment of connubial bliss. Aligning this with Buddhism yields an allusion to the third emptiness, emptiness of the internal and external. In terms of Tantric Buddhist practice, this illustrates the principle that realization of inner and outer emptiness is a necessary concomitant of engagement in the transformation of connubial bliss into spiritual practice.

The fourth stage of life, in conventional Hindu usage, is the stage of liberation, when one leaves society to contemplate the eternal and prepare for physical death. Aligned with the fourth emptiness of Buddhism, this yields an illustration of the principle of parinirvana, ultimate extinction.

The girl who is egolessness at heart is the essence of emptiness. Always symbolized by a female, here emptiness is represented as a girl to emphasize the sense of innocence, as the void upon void of the emptiness of emptiness is innocent of any notion, even of emptiness. That is the true nature of egolessness.

The Buddhist principle of emptiness is thoroughly rational, but the rational principle coincides with direct experience and intuitive insight. Without the inner formless insight into essence, the outer formal knowledge of the principle of emptiness cannot be effective. Therefore it is said that the girl is well protected while awake, just as true emptiness as such can only be realized by conscious experience.

Untie, release the vexatious knot
of illusion and delusion!
Frolicking in great ecstasy,
the Wild Man has taken the Void to wife.

This couplet uses conventional terminology of Hinayana, Mahayana, *and* Vajrayana Buddhism all together to construct a colorful illustration of the principle that "nirvana cannot be attained without arriving at ultimate truth." Thus the "wild man" of free use of expedient means needs to marry the "void" and be released in the "ecstasy" of transconceptual insight in order to realize the aim of ultimate truth and attain liberation from vexation, bondage, illusion and delusion, in nirvana.

Look here! My third house is like space!
How splendid! The cotton is in bloom!

Seeing the third house to be like space again refers in another way to realization of the emptiness of inner and outer emptiness. The cotton blooming is an artful expression that illustrates, in addition to its code meaning, the Buddhist principle of "resorting to conventional usage to express absolute truth."

The word used here in old Bengali for "cotton" is *kapasu.* Using this word rather than the more common *tula* signals uncommon usage, alerting the reader to something else, or some other meaning. The expression "blooming" is a hint to uncovering this meaning, in its sense of "splitting open."

Dividing *kapasu* into two, making *ka-pasu,* yields the meaning "next to *ka.*" In the Sanskrit and Bengali alphabets, "next to *ka*" is *kha.* In the Sanskrit language, from which Hindu and Buddhist Bengali is derived, *kha* means "space." This is a standard symbol for emptiness in Mahayana and Tantric Vajrayana Buddhism. Thus "cotton blooming" stands for the uncovering of the absolute truth of emptiness within the conventional realities of the world.

Use of such a symbolic device, at once artful and yet calm and free of emotional extreme, in a context full of erotic imagery, represents the actual feeling of the experience of emptiness within the experience of artful living.

Beside the third house is the moonlight;
Darkness opened, space blossoms.

The moonlight beside the third house is awareness of the fourth emptiness in the midst of the experience of the third emptiness. The opening of the darkness symbolizes the voiding of voidness, realization of the emptiness of emptiness. The blossoming of space then illustrates the experience of oneness of samsara and nirvana, wherein everything is pure.

The millet is ripened,
the wild man and woman are drunk;
All day long the savage feels naught,
senseless in great ecstasy.

Millet is a cheap grain, signifying plainness and nonadornment, the simplicity of experience in itself, without pretense and artificial rationalization. The ripening of the millet of experience, and its fermentation and distillation into intoxicating liquor, symbolize the development of intense insight into the essence of reality. Intoxication represents the liberation of the mind from the confines of the apparent world as known to ordinary consciousness. Absence of feeling and sense in great ecstasy alludes to the indescribable nature of this transcendental insight and the experience it yields.

The fourth abode is built of basketwork;
Hoisted up on it, the savage has been cremated,
while a virtuous she-jackal cries.

The relative flimsiness of basketwork stands for the impermanence of the body and the individual life in the world. This is the reason, in conventional terms, for entrance into the fourth stage of life, liberation, in preparation for physical death.

The relative airiness of basketwork stands for experience of the ultimate emptiness of the conditional world, both subjective and objective, both inside and outside ourselves. In Buddhist terms, this is the fourth emptiness, void upon void. This is also the basis of parinirvana.

The cremation of the savage in the fourth abode represents the transcendence of subtle residual attachments to the experience of unity of samsara and nirvana. It also represents parinirvana.

The she-jackal of empty egolessness cries when the savage of expedient means is cremated, because "without resorting to conventional usage, ultimate truth cannot be expressed."

The one intoxicated with the world has died,
offering to the dead made in the ten directions;
Look—the savage has become inert,
his wildness at an end.

This is a touching description of the end of a Buddha's life on earth, representing the end of a teaching cycle, and the distribution of the Buddha's relics, symbolizing the residual influence of the teachings. Until their future rebirth as a living word, these teachings become a dead word, inert relics with no power to act on their own.

NOTES

1. Cleary. T. *Dhammapada: The Sayings of Buddha* (New York: Bantam Books, 1995), p. 21.

2. Cleary, T. *The Flower Ornament Scripture: A Translation of the Avatamsaka-sutra* (Boston: Shambhala Publications, 1993), p. 1276.

3. *The Flower Ornament Scripture,* pp. 1270–1273.

4. For the sake of the general reader, I have omitted diacritical marks in transcribing Sanskrit names and terms.

5. Cleary, T. *The Original Face: An Anthology of Rinzai Zen* (New York: Grove Press, 1978), p. 41.

6. Cleary, T. *Living a Good Life: Advice on Virtue, Love, and Action from the Ancient Greek Masters* (Boston: Shambhala Publications, 1997), p. 15.

7. *Dhammapada,* pp. 14–15.

8. *The Flower Ornament Scripture,* pp. 306–307.

9. Cleary, T. *The Essential Tao* (San Francisco: HarperSanFrancisco, 1991), p. 57.

10. *Dhammapada,* p. 108.

11. Cleary, T. *Buddhist Yoga: A Comprehensive Course* (Boston: Shambhala Publications, 1995), p. 10.

12. *Buddhist Yoga,* p. 10.

13. *Buddhist Yoga.* p. 10.

14. Cleary, T. *Kensho: The Heart of Zen* (Boston: Shambhala Publications, 1997) p. 75.

15. *Buddhist Yoga,* p. 1.

16. *Buddhist Yoga,* p. 1.

17. *Buddhist Yoga,* p. 10.

18. Cleary, T. *Unlocking the Zen Koan* (Berkeley: North Atlantic Books, 1997), p. 42.

19. Cleary, T. *Immortal Sisters: Secrets of Taoist Women* (Berkeley: North Atlantic Books, 1996), p. 8.

20. *Dhammapada,* p. 35.

21. *Dhammapada,* p. 62.

22. Cleary, T. *Zen Essence: The Science of Freedom* (Boston: Shambhala Publications, 1989), p. 76.

23. *Zen Essence,* p. 26.

24. *Zen Essence,* p. 26.

25. Cleary, T. *Entry into the Inconceivable: An Introduction to Hua-yen Buddhism* (Honolulu: University of Hawaii Press, 1983). p. 162.

26. Cleary, T. *The Secret of the Golden Flower* (San Francisco: HarperSanFrancisco, 1991), pp. 23-24.

27. *Buddhist Yoga,* p. 29.

28. *The Secret of the Golden Flower,* p. 37.

29. *The Secret of the Golden Flower,* p. 13.

30. *The Secret of the Golden Flower,* p. 13.

31. *Dhammapada,* p. 125.

32. *Dhammapada,* p. 56.

33. *Dhammapada,* p. 51.

34. Cleary, T. *Living and Dying with Grace* (Boston: Shamhala Publications, 1995), pp. 23–24.

35. *Dhammapada,* pp. 50–51.

36. *Dhammapada,* p. 45.

37. *Living and Dying with Grace,* p. 68.

38. *The Flower Ornament Scripture,* p. 300.

39. *Buddhist Yoga,* p. 18.

40. *The Flower Ornament Scripture,* p. 299.

41. *Zen Essence,* p. 31.

42. *Zen Essence,* p. 61.

43. *Buddhist Yoga,* p. 29.

44. *Buddhist Yoga,* p. 34.

45. *Buddhist Yoga,* p. 10.

46. Cleary, T. *Shobogenzo: Zen Essays by Dogen* (Honolulu: University of Hawaii Press, 1986), p. 39.

47. *Dhammapada,* p. 41.

48. *The Flower Ornament Scripture,* p. 704.

49. Cleary T. *Instant Zen: Waking up in the Present* (Berkeley: North Atlantic Books, 1994), p. 74.

50. *Instant Zen,* p. 80.

51. *Dhammapada,* p. 113.

52. *Zen Essence,* p. 53.

53. *Buddhist Yoga,* p. 28.

54. *Buddhist Yoga,* p. 30.

55. *Instant Zen,* p. 129.

56. *Entry into the Inconceivable,* p. 145.

57. *Dhammapada,* pp. 7–8.

58. *Buddhist Yoga,* p. 37.

59. *Buddhist Yoga,* pp. 24–25.

60. *Zen Essence,* p. 79.

61. *Buddhist Yoga,* p. 21.

62. *Shobogenzo,* p. *32.*

63. Cleary, T. and Cleary, J. C. *The Blue Cliff Record* (Boston: Shambhala Publications, 1977), p. 240.

64. *Dhammapada,* p. 127.

65. Cleary, T. *Vitality, Energy, Spirit: A Taoist Sourcebook* (Boston: Shambhala Publications, 1991). p. 95.

66. *Dhammapada,* p. 17.

67. *The Flower Ornament Scripture,* p. 767.

68. *Vitality, Energy, Spirit,* p. 91.

69. *The Flower Ornament Scripture,* p. 765.

70. *The Flower Ornament Scripture,* pp. 880–881.

71. *Zen Essence,* p. 79.

72. *The Blue Cliff Record,* p. 489.

73. *Buddhist Yoga,* p. 30.

74. *Unlocking the Zen Koan,* p. 95.

75. Cleary, T. *Rational Zen: The Mind of Dogen Zenji* (Boston: Shambhala Publications, 1993), p. 44.

76. *The Flower Ornament Scripture,* p. 881.

77. *Rational Zen,* p. 43.

78. *The Flower Ornament Scripture,* p. 885.

79. *Zen Essence,* p. 16.

80. *Zen Essence,* p. 51.

81. *Rational Zen,* p. 63.

82. Cleary, T. *Practical Taoism* (Boston: Shambhala Publications, 1996), p. 3.

83. Cleary, T. *The Book of Leadership and Strategy: Lessons of the Chinese Masters* (Boston: Shambhala Publications, 1992), p. 112.

84. *Practical Taoism,* p. 27.

85. *The Book of Leadership and Strategy,* p. 113.

86. *The Flower Ornament Scripture,* p. 291.

87. *The Flower Ornament Scripture,* p. 378.

88. *The Flower Ornament Scripture,* p. 379.

89. *The Flower Ornament Scripture,* p. 381.

90. *Rational Zen,* p. 57.

91. *The Flower Ornament Scripture,* p. 707.

92. *The Flower Ornament Scripture,* p. 871.

93. *The Flower Ornament Scripture,* p. 881.

94. *Buddhist Yoga,* p. 1.

95. *Zen Essence,* p. 74.

96. *Rational Zen,* p. 59.

97. *Rational Zen,* p. 53.

Supplementary Notes

a) cf. Kamenetz, Rodger, *The Jew in the Lotus* (San Francisco: HarperSanFrancisco, 1994), p. 213.

b) cf. Scott, Ernest, *The People of the Secret* (London: Octagon Press, 1983), pp. 261–262.

c) On the main Sufi orders and their ways, see Shah, ldries, *The Way of the Sufi* (London: Octagon Press, 1968).

d) On the system of subtleties, see Shah, ldries, *The Sufis* (New York: Doubleday, 1964), p. 430; and Shah, ldries, *A Perfumed Scorpion* (London: Octagon Press, 1978), pp. 89–90.

SELECT BIBLIOGRAPHY

Bagchi, Jhunu. *The History and Culture of the Palas of Bengal and Bihar.* New Delhi: Abhinav Publications, 1993.

Chatterji, Suniti Kumar. *The Origin and Development of the Bengali Language.* London: George Allen & Unwin, 1970.

Chattopadhyay, Bhaskar, ed. *Culture of Bengal through the Ages: Some Aspects.* Burdwan, West Bengal: University of Burdwan, 1988.

Cleary, Thomas. *Buddhist Yoga: A Comprehensive Course.* Boston: Shambhala, 1995.

———. *Dhammapada: The Sayings of Buddha.* New York: Bantam Books, 1995.

———. *Entry into the Inconceivable: An Introduction to Hua-yen Buddhism.* Honolulu: University of Hawaii Press, 1983.

———. *The Flower Ornament Scripture: A Translation of the Avatamsaka-sutra.* Boston: Shambhala, 1984, 1986, 1987, 1989, 1993.

———. *No Barrier: Unlocking the Zen Koan.* New York: Bantam, 1993.

———. *Rational Zen: The Mind of Dagen Zenji.* Boston: Shambhala, 1992.

———. *The Secret of the Golden Flower.* San Francisco: HarperSan Francisco, 1991.

———. *Shobogenzo: Zen Essays by Dogen.* Honolulu: University of Hawaii Press, 1986.

———. *Vitality, Energy, Spirit: A Taoist Sourcebook.* Boston: Shambhala, 1991.

———. *Zen Essence: The Science of Freedom.* Boston: Shambhala, 1989.

Cleary, Thomas and J. C. Cleary. *The Blue Cliff Record.* Boston: Shambhala, 1977.

Dudjom Rinpoche. *The Nyingma School of Tibetan Buddhism.* Boston: Wisdom Publications, 1991.

(Mukhapadhyay) Mukherji, Tarapad. *The Old Bengali Language and Text.* Calcutta: Calcutta University, 1967.

Scott, Ernest. *The People of the Secret.* London: Octagon Press, 1983.

Sen, Nilratan, ed. *Caryagitikos.* West Bengal: Dipali Sen, 1978.

Sen, Sukumar. *An Etymological Dictionary of Bengali: c. 1000–1800.* Calcutta: Eastern Publishers, 1971.

Shah, ldries. *The Way of the Sufi.* London: Octagon Press, 1968.

Yoshida, Keikoh. *Kon-Tai Ryobu Shingon Kaiki.* Kyoto: Heirakuji Shoten, 1971.

ABOUT THE TRANSLATOR

Thomas Cleary is an internationally known translator of spiritual classics from Chinese, Japanese, Sanskrit, Pali, and Arabic. He holds a BA in Far Eastern Languages from Harvard College and MA and PhD degrees in East Asian Languages and Civilizations from Harvard University.

JAICO PUBLISHING HOUSE

Elevate Your Life. Transform Your World.

ESTABLISHED IN 1946, Jaico Publishing House is home to world-transforming authors such as Sri Sri Paramahansa Yogananda, Osho, the Dalai Lama, Sri Sri Ravi Shankar, Sadhguru, Robin Sharma, Deepak Chopra, Jack Canfield, Eknath Easwaran, Devdutt Pattanaik, Khushwant Singh, John Maxwell, Brian Tracy, and Stephen Hawking.

Our late founder Mr. Jaman Shah first established Jaico as a book distribution company. Sensing that independence was around the corner, he aptly named his company Jaico ('Jai' means victory in Hindi). In order to service the significant demand for affordable books in a developing nation, Mr. Shah initiated Jaico's own publications. Jaico was India's first publisher of paperback books in the English language.

While self-help, religion and philosophy, mind/body/spirit, and business titles form the cornerstone of our non-fiction list, we publish an exciting range of travel, current affairs, biography, and popular science books as well. Our renewed focus on popular fiction is evident in our new titles by a host of fresh young talent from India and abroad. Jaico's recently established translations division translates selected English content into nine regional languages.

Jaico distributes its own titles. With its headquarters in Mumbai, Jaico has branches in Ahmedabad, Bangalore, Chennai, Delhi, Hyderabad, and Kolkata.

SINCE 1946